D1071061

THE LACKAWANNA STORY

The
LACKAWANNA
Story

THE FIRST HUNDRED YEARS OF
THE DELAWARE, LACKAWANNA
AND WESTERN RAILROAD

by Robert J. Casey and W. A. S. Douglas

McGraw-Hill Book Company, Inc.

NEW YORK   LONDON   TORONTO

THE LACKAWANNA STORY

Published by the McGraw-Hill Book Company, Inc.
Printed in the United States of America

TO THE EMPLOYEES
PAST AND PRESENT
OF THE DELAWARE, LACKAWANNA AND
WESTERN RAILROAD
WHOSE TOIL HAS MADE POSSIBLE
THIS HUNDRED-YEAR RECORD

Contents

Part I: THE RAILROAD

1   *King Charles's Grant*

THE giant towers of New York shimmer in the early morning sun. The sidewalks are thronged with thousands of workers hurrying to thousands of offices and other places of business. The subways disgorge other thousands; the buses empty their sardine-packed loads.

Over the cluttered expanse of the Hudson River a transatlantic liner is being noisily nosed to her dock by impatient tugs; another giant of the sea is being similarly pushed into the start of her journey eastward. Back and forth, over the river, ply the ferryboats of the Delaware, Lackawanna and Western Railroad, bringing suburban customers into the daily grind—35,000 people being hauled off to work in the morning; the same 35,000 going back home in the evening; thousands of others riding the Lackawanna to the great metropolis to shop, to transact business, to seek pleasure. Sleek through trains arrive and depart at the Hoboken Terminal night and day.

At the freight depots the trains of commerce come and go, hauling coal, bituminous and anthracite, hauling general merchandise, manufactured articles, farm produce, machinery.

All this had its beginnings a hundred years ago, after the discovery of hard coal and iron deposits in the region that included the tiny settlements of Slocum's Hollow, now the hustling city of Scranton. There they had lain, coal and iron, to be had for the digging. Cabins could be developed into towns, villages into cities. If fuel could be moved, factories would arise; if the iron could be turned into rails, a railroad could be laid down; the railroad could haul the coal. It was as simple and as complicated as that.

But first there was the colonial wilderness.

Charles II, King of England, gave away the northeastern corner of what is now Pennsylvania three times.

On the first occasion, in the summer of 1662, "the Merrie Monarch" gave audience to John Winthrop, governor of the colony of Connecticut, and granted a charter covering acreage as impressive as that of the Louisiana Purchase.

The Connecticut Claim, as it came to be called, consisted of all the land between the forty-first and forty-second degrees of north latitude and extended from Narragansett Bay to the sea—which meant the Pacific Ocean. The King's gift narrows down to a strip a trifle over 68 miles in width, running from Rhode Island to Oregon and California. As places "already settled" were left out, the present really began on the right bank of the Delaware River, which is the boundary line between the present states of New Jersey and Pennsylvania, and ended somewhere between what is now Eureka, California, and Medford, Oregon.

A princely gift, indeed, as things go today! The hitch in it was that what are now Pennsylvania, Ohio, Indiana, Illinois, Iowa, Nebraska, Wyoming, Idaho, Nevada, Utah, California, and Oregon were unexplored and fairly full of hostile Indians. The governor of Connecticut bade "Old Rowley" a seemingly appreciative farewell, came home, and tucked the grant away among the colony's souvenirs. It gathered dust for ninety-one years.

In 1681, William Penn, the Quaker who had already begun settlement of New Jersey by people of his faith, came to King Charles for a favor. Penn rightly deserved the King's good will. He had been mainly instrumental in quelling what might well have been another English civil war. His masterly pamphlets, "Epistle to the Children of Light in this Generation," "An Address to Protestants of all Persuasions," and "One Project for the Good of England," had calmed Englishmen of all religious persuasions, brought about the impeachment of corrupt ministers and councilors, established set periods for the sittings of Parliament, and started the enactment of laws for religious freedom.

William Penn wanted from his monarch "a tract of land in America north of Maryland, bounded on the east by the Delaware River, calling a western limit on Maryland, and northward as far as plantable [*i.e.*, available for immigration]."

Cecilius Calvert, second Lord Baltimore, who had inherited the Maryland concession (1632) from his father, George, the first Baron, got wind of William Penn's request from his friend, James, Duke of York, the King's brother (later King James II). York wanted an American concession, not to do any settling himself, but to peddle off tracts to wealthy adventurers. Word had come to London that the region desired by the Quaker leader was even more richly fertile than the province of New York. Both the Duke of York and Lord Baltimore protested angrily to the King.

Easy-going Charles, as was frequently the case when he was in a quandary, sought the advice of his favorite mistress of the moment. The lady happened to be the longest-lasting of his many loves, Nell Gwyn, "Sweet Nell of Old Drury," the former London street urchin and orange-seller who became the best-loved comedienne of the Restoration. She told Charles that she would like to meet the Quaker.

So William Penn, when he came to the private audience at Whitehall Palace, was surprised to find it hardly private. Curled up in an easy chair by one of those great windows, from which she could, if so minded, look down on the spot where her royal lover's father had been beheaded, was Nell Gwyn.

The star of *The English Monsieur*, of *Secret Love* and of *Flora's Vagaries* stared up at the big Quaker, a strange type of man to her. The usual twinkle had gone from her blue eyes; her lovely red hair, worn long, was combed discreetly over dimpled shoulders, concealing an otherwise startling décolleté. Mistress Gwyn, who had been rebuffed by more than one with the effrontery to consider himself an arbiter of the morals of others, saw Will Penn as another self-appointed critic and carried a chip on her shoulder. Black Charles, well aware of her mood, wore his malicious grin, lounged in a chaise longue, and hoped for fireworks. The Quaker entered, made a knee, stood erect.

Charles nodded, waved his beringed left hand in the direction of the lovely little bundle by the window.

"Mistress Gwyn, Master Penn," was all he said.

The big solemn man skirted the chaise longue where sprawled the King, approached Nell Gwyn with a smile—something she had not looked for from a Quaker face to face with a light o' love. Instinctively, she stretched out her hand. Penn took the tiny, perfumed paw between huge finger and thumb, pressed it to his lips.

"Doubtless," observed Charles who had watched every move, "you have seen Mistress Nell in one of her plays."

If his intention had been to embarrass Penn, there was a distinct failure. The Quaker launched into careful praise and sound criticism of both Beaumont and Fletcher's *Philaster* and Sir Robert Howard's *Surprisal*. He delighted Nell when he reproached his monarch with selfishness for his refusal to permit his favorite regularly to tread the boards at Drury Lane.

"Let me hear your project for the extension of my dominions through peaceful penetration," said the King. "But sit you down, Master Penn."

In the royal anteroom, Cecilius, Lord Baltimore, paced the floor for an hour and more. Warned by the Duke of York of Penn's audience, he had hoped to inject himself into the meeting to argue for his "rights." The request had been denied, but he was hoping that nothing would be signed before his friend, York, could reach his royal brother.

Baltimore, tired of tramping, had just jerked himself angrily into a chair when the big Quaker walked past, signed parchment in hand. Charles had made but one change in the wording of the document.

"Sylvania?" he had said, noting the name Penn had chosen for the colony. "A pretty name. But honor where honor is due, Master Penn. We will call it Pennsylvania."

The King had completely forgotten all about the Connecticut settlers and their previous grant "from sea to sea."

Charles's third gift of Pennsylvania acres came soon after Penn's visit. Nell Gwyn's mother, the widow of a soldier, was inclined to the bottle. Her daughter had bought her a cottage in Chelsea, close to that stretch of ground where the King—on his favorite's insistence—was building a home for disabled veterans of his armies, the first veterans' home in the world. Old Mrs. Gwyn, following one of her daughter's frequent absences at Whitehall, had fallen into a pond and drowned. Nell was inconsolable. Her mother had gone and she feared that her King would eventually tire of her. As she pointed out, he tired of so many.

"For you, Nell," grinned the cynical monarch, "not till God calls me; and methinks I hear the trumpets."

(He had but two more years to live.)

"When that happens," sobbed the little courtesan, "I shall go far, far away and take our two sons with me. James (the Duke of York) has no use for me or for them."

Charles, ever the cynic, considered this sound reasoning. About as far away as Nell could get, he observed, would be to Master Penn's acreage in Pennsylvania. He called in Jermyn, his secretary, and while Nell sobbed and the King guffawed, there was prepared for Mistress Gwyn "a grant of twenty thousand acres of the land judged by Master Penn the most fertile between the rivers of the Delaware and the Susquehannock [Susquehanna] and most adjacent to my province of New York."

Nell Gwyn never went to Pennsylvania, never even took legal possession of a grant which William Penn would have been delighted to honor. Given (much to her astonishment) a generous pension by her lover's brother, King James, and adored by her two sons, she spent the years left her after Charles's death in kindly work among the old soldiers of the Chelsea Hospital, the erection of which she had brought about. The document which granted her a portion of northeastern Pennsylvania is said to have remained in the possession of her oldest son, the first Duke of St. Albans, and of his descendants until it was accidentally destroyed by fire during the eighteenth century.

Despite the fact that William Penn was absolute "proprietor" of Pennsylvania, it was his scrupulous rule to pay Indian tribes for the lands he decided were to be colonized. According to Voltaire, the Quaker's Great Treaty of 1683 was "the only treaty not sworn to and never broken." This condition lasted until his death in 1719, and during his thirty-seven years of rule, Pennsylvania became a haven for the oppressed and the persecuted of many lands.

Here came the Quakers from Wales and western England; the German Mennonites under Pastorius—as devout, as bold, as tolerant as Penn; Lutherans from the Palatinate; Moravians from Bohemia; and in great droves the Presbyterian Scotch-Irish. These latter, holding as tenants the lands of the Catholic northern Irish, which had been seized three-quarters of a century before, were suffering from brutal annual rent increases by their landlords, the descendants of those younger sons of Scottish chiefs who were granted proprietary rights in Ulster by James I in the "settlement" of 1609.

In the summer of 1753 a number of prominent citizens of Connecticut, Rhode Island, and Massachusetts, assembled at Windham, Connecticut, for the purpose of discussing a ninety-one-year-old document on faded "royal" parchment. Discovered by some clerk and bearing the signature of Charles II, King of England "and the lands beyond the seas called the Royal American Colonies," the document granted to the Connecticut Colony proprietary rights to a 68-mile-wide strip across North America "from sea to sea."

The gentlemen from Connecticut, Rhode Island, and Massachusetts were interested only in colonizing a comparatively small portion of this vast acreage (then known as the Wyoming Region and the Wyoming Valley) lying between the Delaware and Susquehanna rivers, bounded on the north by the province of New York and on the south by a straight line between what is now Stroudsburg on the New Jersey border and the left bank of the Susquehanna River.

The Windham convention arrived at the conclusion that certain proprietary rights were involved and formed the Susquehanna Company for the prosecution, if necessary, of those rights. Two years later, a similar project was launched at Hartford under the name of the Delaware Company. But in the ensuing attempts at colonization the Susquehanna Company did all the spadework.

Pennsylvania was still a vaguely bounded province when the Windham convention met in 1753. The Maryland-Delaware line had been laid down in 1750 by decree of Lord Chancellor Hardwicke, but not until 1763, after a trifle of bloodshed between the Marylanders and the Delawareans, was the Mason-Dixon survey undertaken to establish the Pennsylvania-Maryland boundaries. In 1784 Virginia was to agree to an extension of the Mason-Dixon line for the establishment of the western boundary of Pennsylvania at a meridian drawn from a point on the line five degrees of longitude west of the Delaware River. The forty-second parallel was to be finally selected as the northern boundary of the state in 1789, after Congress had decided against the claims of the men from Connecticut.

But a lot of water from the Delaware River was to flow past the New World's greatest city, Philadelphia, and a lot of blood was to flow from the veins of Connecticut men and Pennsylvania men before the former, victors in the field, were to lose their case in the halls of Congress. The Pennamite War was America's first civil war.

"These Quakers won't fight," announced John Davenport, of New Haven, grandson of one of the men in the entourage of Governor Winthrop at the time of King Charles's grant. "I do not mean that they are lacking in courage, but their ways are the ways of peace and of fair-mindedness. We are getting crowded here, and our rocky soil is not to be compared with the lush richness of the Wyoming Valley. We shall pay the Indians for their land, as was always the fair procedure followed by William Penn. The inhabitants of the City of Brotherly Love will not question our undeniable rights to a tiny portion of what was given us."

In July of 1754, following a "preliminary survey" in the region of the Delaware Water Gap by a "journeying committee" from Colchester, Connecticut, a delegation of Connecticut, Rhode Island, and Massachusetts men, representing the Susquehanna Company, met with the chiefs of the Six Nations at Albany, New York. The Indian chiefs claiming suzerainty were offered and accepted the sum of £2,000, for which they signed the deed known as "the Susquehanna Purchase." This granted to the Susquehanna Company the land alongside the north branch of the Susquehanna River from the mouth of Nescopeck Creek, 22 miles southwest of Wilkes-Barre, to the Pennsylvania–New York boundary line, and extending a distance of about 15 miles from the river, east and west. The right of the six chiefs to sell was later disputed by other chiefs.*

The Seven Years' War between Austria, France, Russia, Sweden, and Saxony on one side and Prussia and England on the other (1756–1763) halted the plans of the upholders of the Connecticut

* WEYBURN, S. FLETCHER, *Following the Connecticut Trail*, The Anthracite Press.

Claim to settle northeastern Pennsylvania under both Charles's charter and the Albany purchase. England and France were fighting both a maritime and a colonial war, which actually, in so far as America was concerned, began in 1754, when the French threw a string of forts along the Ohio Valley. George Washington, then an English colonel, built Fort Duquesne (Pittsburgh), only to have it taken from him by the French, whom he later defeated at Mountain Meadows. Shortly after, he was forced by an overwhelming army to surrender at a hastily thrown-up breastwork called Fort Necessity. Following the capitulation, he and his troops were released.

On July 15, 1755, General Edward Braddock, Washington's commander, sought to recapture Fort Duquesne, but his column was cut to pieces, and he himself died gallantly on the battlefield. Three years later, General Forbes recaptured Fort Duquesne and renamed it Fort Pitt after the English prime minister. With the fall of Quebec (September 31, 1759), all Pennsylvania came into English hands. But those war years, the men of Connecticut rightly decided, were not the times for peaceful penetration.

In the middle of August, 1762, 109 settlers registered with the Susquehanna Company at Windham, and, led by Stephen Gardner, John Jenkins, and John Smith, set out to occupy the Wyoming lands. The rest bore typical New England names—Baldwin, Comstock, Atherton, Hollister, Dorrance, etc. They rode horseback; their equipment consisted of blankets, firearms, food, clothing, and axes. They crossed the Hudson River at Fishkill and passed through Orange County to the Delaware River. They entered Pennsylvania near the mouth of the Lackawaxen Creek, following Indian trails, and finally encamped at what is now the town of Shickshinny on the Delaware, Lackawanna, and Western Railroad about 25 miles southwest of Scranton. Here they were visited by Teedyuscung, King of the Delawares, who had insisted that the Albany purchase had been illegally obtained, and warned to get out. The settlers stayed.

In the spring of 1763 the first women and children of the Connecticut Colony, led by Parshall Terry, moved in. Their trek was accomplished with horses and wagons, a road having been hacked through the forests by a project for which the Susquehanna Company had appropriated the magnificent sum of £30! Almost at the time of their arrival King Teedyuscung died in a fire in his hut —the result, it was said, of a drunken debauch. But his complaint had been forwarded by the proprietors of Pennsylvania to the English government, and as a result Governor Fitch of Connecticut was advised by London to "halt all proceedings pending a settlement." By this time the colonists had dug in from Shickshinny to Mill Creek, now part of Wilkes-Barre.

On the afternoon of Saturday, October 15, 1763, the Delaware warriors, led by Captain Bull, eldest son of Teedyuscung, swooped down on the settlement and slaughtered or took prisoner two-thirds of the colonists and put the torch to their cabins. The survivors made their way back through the wilderness to Connecticut. The Wyoming Valley again became an Indian hunting ground, and neither the Pennsylvania proprietors nor the English government in London seemed to be unduly disturbed over the massacre.

It is a hard thing, indeed—and the conclusion has been proved many times since the landing of the Pilgrims—to deprive a Connecticut man of his presumed rights. Again and again groups of New Englanders moved into Wyoming, despite still another "purchase" from the Indians—this time executed in favor of Richard and Thomas Penn, sons of William. The Penns divided the "purchase" into manors, along the lines laid down by William the Conqueror in his Domesday Book. The lords of the manors could rent or sell to colonists and lay out townsites. Western and southern Pennsylvanians and other immigrants moved into the lands east of the Susquehanna, encroaching on what the Susquehanna Company and the Delaware Company considered theirs. The settlers under the Penns called themselves the Pennamites; the men from Connecticut were known as the Yankees.

The first military gesture in the first of the two Pennamite wars was made by Major John Durkee, the founder of Wilkes-Barre, after twenty settlers had been arrested for refusal to get off "Pennamite land." He took command of a troop of 140 Connecticut horsemen, rode through the forests, and made camp at the Big Bend of the Susquehanna River. Charles Stewart, representative and lessor of Penn lands, wrote to Governor Richard Penn at Philadelphia that his lands had been "invaded by gentry of the very lowest class, armed and fit for mischief." Colonel Turbott Francis took command of the Pennamites.

Governor Penn issued a proclamation calling on Durkee and his troopers to evacuate Pennsylvania. Connecticut's reply was to add 150 more horsemen to the major's command, and Durkee proceeded to erect a stockade. This was called Fort Durkee and stood in what is now the center of Wilkes-Barre. The Yankee farmers who had been arrested had been held at Easton. They were finally granted bail and later released. Fifteen joined Durkee in his stockade, while five returned to their farms.

The story of the Pennamite-Yankee wars is that of sporadic bloody raids on each other's settlements and fortifications. The Pennamites were on several such occasions assisted by Indians, who lent horror to the battles by torture (scalpings and mutilations). Both sides took prisoners, and if the records of Captain (later Colonel) Zebulon Butler, commander at Fort Wyoming, are to be taken as read, white Pennamite hostages were at least treated not too badly. For example, in September, 1770, Captain Butler billed the Susquehanna Company as follows:

Paid T. French for whiskey during siege . . . three pounds, eleven shillings, sixpence.
Paid Mead for whiskey . . . thirty shillings.
Same, twenty gallons rum . . . five pounds.
Paid George Estey for powder . . . thirty shillings.
Three barrels flour for prisoners . . . thirty shillings.
One quart whiskey for raising guardhouse . . . seven shillings.

The first Pennamite-Yankee war ended June 2, 1773, when agreement was made between the Pennsylvania proprietors and the Susquehanna Company that settlements by the latter should remain as they were as of that date and that, from there on, further land applications should be made to Pennsylvania. On May 6, 1775, Captain Butler raised the Twenty-fourth (or Westmoreland) Regiment of the Continental Militia, made up of the Yankees settled in the Wyoming Valley, was appointed its colonel, and marched off to war. The Pennamites contributed to the cause of the Revolution, but not in such numbers.

On September 28 of that year, the Pennamites opened the second war with the Yankees by attacking what was left of the settlers on the west branch of the Susquehanna, killing and wounding more than a score and taking a dozen prisoners. On September 4 the Continental Congress ordered the province of Pennsylvania to halt Pennamite raids on the Yankee women and children, half-grown youths, and old men. The edict was tardily obeyed.

On June 29, 1778, Colonel Zebulon Butler, who had returned to the Wyoming Valley from the war, was apprised of the approach of an English force, commanded by Major John Butler (no relation), from the north over the Susquehanna River. This consisted of 400 English regular soldiers known as Butler's Rangers, a detachment from the Royal Greens (Lincolnshire Regiment). The English force was augmented by about 800 Indians from the Seneca, Cayuga, and Delaware tribes. Colonel Butler hurriedly mustered about 400 men and boys and went out to meet the enemy. He fought a gallant rear-guard action till he reached Forty Fort on July 3. Here the Indians were let loose on the Yankees. In the mad massacre which followed, barely a dozen Yankees escaped.

The Connecticut settlers had at last been overwhelmed. Those who were serving in the Continental Army in other parts of the country had the scant satisfaction of learning that, although the High Court at Trenton had upheld the Pennsylvania claim, they could retain the acreage they had cleared. In 1789 the Congress of the United States approved the conclusions of the Trenton High Court.

2 *The Slocums*

In the 1762 and subsequent incursions into the Wyoming Region by the Connecticut men, the trail traveled between the Delaware and Lackawanna rivers was the Shohola Minisink Path, so known to generations of Indians before the advent of the white man. It led out of Wyoming, eastward to Coshutunk (Cochecton) on the shores of the upper Delaware. This trail followed the eastern bank of the Lackawanna River to Springbrook, Stafford Meadow, and Nay Aug, or Roaring Brook—this last part of the present location of Scranton—and passed through the Indian village of Capouse.

At Capouse, the trail broke into two paths, one leading off to Oquaga (now Windsor), New York, through Ligett's Gap (also variously spelled "Leggett's," etc.) and the Abington Wilderness, while the other, heading east, plunged into the forest and traversed the present site of Dunmore, passed over the mountain slope, and crossed the Moosic Range. Along this track, with the £30 (English) donated by the Susquehanna Company, the first crude wagon road was hacked open from the Hudson River to Wyoming Valley. Manageable by either pack horse or wheeled vehicle, it was the most direct rout from Connecticut to the backwoods of Lackawanna and Wyoming.

This territory was called Westmoreland by the Connecticut Yankees as they began to people it. By 1771 the Susquehanna Company had surveyed six towns: Wilkes-Barre, Nanticoke (Hanover),

Pittstown (Pittston), Plymouth, The Forty (Kingston), Capouse Meadows (later Providence). A town, in the terms of the Connecticut settlers, could range in size from half an acre to half of what today might be a state of the union. The town of Capouse Meadows, or Providence, is today the rich and fertile Lackawanna Valley.

As both the words "Delaware" and "Lackawanna" are of deep importance to the subject of this book, it might be well to clear up their meaning. "Delaware," as we know, derives from the tribe of that name, which, originally the Leni-Lenape, took the name of Lord De La Warr, its first white overlord. "Lackawanna," in Delaware Indian, meant "the forks of a stream." The word began to appear in surveys, sales, grants, transfers, etc., following the first trek of the Connecticut men, and is shown in various spellings such as "Lackawanick," "Lackawaneck," "Lackawannuck," "Lackawanny," "Leghawanny." After the Wyoming Massacre the army expedition through the region, led by General John Sullivan, broke all Indian power in northeastern Pennsylvania, and soldier-settlers, heirs to slaughtered settlers, new adventurers, and former absentee owners moved in. The spelling then was officially recorded as "Lackawanna."

Forward-looking men began to eye the well-watered Lackawanna Valley with a view to the erection of sawmills, gristmills, and forges. Years of comparative peace and agricultural development descended upon the region. Trees were felled for lumber, and their stumps were blown out to prepare fields for grain. Tools were needed for the construction of farmhouses and town houses, and implements for the planting and harvesting of crops. The hardy pioneers needed something else, too—whiskey.

Probably the most forward-looking young man of those forward-looking young men who saw, early in the settlement of the Lackawanna Valley, what the settlers would most need was Ebenezer Slocum, who decided to supply them with all four of their essentials —a sawmill, a gristmill, an iron foundry, and a distillery. On the site of his accumulated and successful endeavors stands today a large portion of the city of Scranton. The Slocum name is also linked with an amazing item of historical American romance and tragedy.

What manner of homes were these which the pioneers from the Old World and from the New erected in these hard-won valley lands, fairly secure from marauding Indians, the quarrel laid at last between the men of Connecticut and the men of Pennsylvania? This was the first great inward penetration; as space is measured today, it was but a few scant miles from the seaboard.

Life was primitive, most primitive. There were some stone houses, but these were few; mostly homes were log cabins, built slowly and laboriously by the settler and his wife and children, if any. Sometimes neighbors gathered together, if neighbors were at all accessible, and helped to build the first rude home on freshly cleared sites. These people were isolated, living in inaccessible and remote spots; the roads were poor, or there were no roads at all. Conditions were hard, and privations and discomforts abounded.

All this was civilization in the making.

Wayland F. Dunaway, in *The Scotch-Irish of Colonial Pennsylvania*, pays a tribute to the wives of Pennsylvania settlers, a tribute which belongs as much to Connecticut Quakeress, German *hausfrau*, Welsh, English, or French bride as it does to his rosy-cheeked Ulster "rain-girl" (so-called because of the beautiful complexion attributed to the continuous soft rain of the old country):

She baked her own bread and did the family cooking, washing and sewing; she milked the cows and churned the butter; she picked, dyed and carded the wool, broke and carded the flax, spun and wove the cloth, cut out the garments and made the family wardrobe. Furthermore, she reared the children, taught them to read and instructed them in the principles of Christianity.

When anyone in the family was sick, she was the nurse and the doctor —with homemade remedies of sulphate of iron, green copperas, bear's oil, snake root and poultices. Mills were scarce and, at first, non-existent; hence, if the housewife wished meal for johnny-cake or corn pone, she had to make it herself from corn ground on the hominy block or in the hand-mills. Cooking utensils were few and cumbersome and there were no labor-saving devices to lighten her work which was not confined entirely to the precincts of her cabin.

She often worked the garden and roamed the woods in search of sassafras, sage and mint to brew into teas. In summer, aided by the smaller children, she picked the wild fruits of the forest—blackberries, plums, cherries, haws, whortleberries, strawberries and grapes. In autumn she laid in stores of hickory nuts and walnuts. In rush seasons she assisted in harvesting the crops, in burning brush and logs and in gathering the fruits of the orchard. Supplies must be laid in to keep the family going through the long winter months and she was kept busy drying apples, making oil from bear or possum fat, hanging corn on the rafters to dry and making corncob molasses.

Her life was a ceaseless round of household duties and domestic cares, of loneliness and drudgery, often resulting in wearing herself out and becoming prematurely old. Moreover, she suffered much anxiety for fear that rations would not last through the winter; that the wolves or other wild animals, would destroy her loved ones if she ventured from home; or that the Indians would swoop down on the household with massacres, burnings and widespread devastation.

In emergencies, especially if her husband were absent in the wars, she learned to mold bullets and to use the rifle to defend her home and fireside from the savages. Her dauntless spirit rose with danger and her heroism equalled that of her husband. The part played by the wife and mother in the life of the American frontier has never been adequately portrayed and perhaps could not be, so great it was and so sublime. On some towering mountain peak of Pennsylvania the Commonwealth should erect to her a monument as a worthy memorial of her character and deeds.*

Wholly such a wife and mother as Mr. Dunaway describes was Ruth Tripp Slocum, wife of Jonathan Slocum, one of the Connecticut settlers, and mother of ten children. One of them, Ebenezer, became the Lackawanna Valley's industrial pioneer. A daughter, Frances, was kidnapped by the Miami Indians under her helpless mother's eyes.

Jonathan Slocum, member of an English Quaker family which had settled in Massachusetts in 1636, was born in East Greenwich, Rhode Island, May 1, 1733. By trade he was a blacksmith. In 1757 he married Ruth Tripp, daughter of Isaac Tripp, a member of the directing committee of the "First Forty" settlers sent out to the Wyoming Region by the Susquehanna Company. Slocum accompanied his father-in-law on this inspection. In the spring of 1771 Tripp returned, built a cabin, and took up land in Capouse Meadows within the present boundaries of the city of Scranton. A hale and

* DUNAWAY, WAYLAND F., *The Scotch-Irish of Colonial Pennsylvania*, University of North Carolina Press, Chapel Hill.

hearty old man, he had already outlived two wives and had but recently wedded a third when, in the fall of 1777, he advised his son-in-law, Jonathan, to return for good to Wyoming.

The Slocums were parents of nine children, the eldest of whom was only eighteen and the youngest a babe in arms when the summons came; their tenth child, Jonathan, was the only one to be born in the new settlement. Their journey, by wagon and six horses, was first proof of a family courage and hardihood which through generations has made the name Slocum revered in northeastern Pennsylvania. The family settled in Wilkes-Barre, where the breadwinner pursued his trade of blacksmith and, with the help of his young sons, farmed a stretch of flat land on the edge of the settlement.

Jonathan Slocum, a conscientious Quaker, was opposed to strife and bloodshed. When news came of the advance into Pennsylvania from New York of the combined force of British soldiers and Indians (preceding the Massacre of Wyoming), he remained at his home. The fact that his wife was to have her tenth child may have been the stubborn, courageous man's reason for staying on his land. The raid by-passed his farm, but after the capitulation of Forty Fort and the massacre, the Slocum family did seek the protection of one of the valley redoubts (Fort Penn). In mid-August, they returned to their home.

On the morning of November 2, 1778—Mrs. Slocum had had her baby six weeks before—Jonathan, with his two boys, William and Benjamin, was at work in the fields almost two miles from the cabin. The eldest son, Giles, was on duty as a soldier at Fort Wyoming. At the Slocum home were Mrs. Slocum; the baby, Jonathan; Judith, aged eighteen; Ebenezer, twelve; Mary, ten; Benjamin, eight; Frances, five; Isaac, three; and Joseph, eighteen months. Living with the Slocums were Mrs. Nathan Kingsley, whose husband had been recently captured by the Indians (he escaped later) and her two teen-age sons.

The Kingsley boys were sharpening knives on a grindstone, and the rest of the family was indoors when, of a sudden, a rifle cracked. Mrs. Slocum rushed to the front door, threw it open to see young Nathan Kingsley, dead, and an Indian about to scalp him with the very knife the youth had been sharpening. Mrs. Slocum snatched her baby from its cot, shouted a warning, and, accompanied by Mrs. Kingsley, fled for the swamp at the back of the house. The younger Kingsley boy made his way into the house; he pushed five-year-old Frances under the stairs and hid there with her. Eighteen-year-old Judith picked up her three-year-old brother, Isaac, and also made for the swamp, while nine-year-old Mary grabbed eighteen-months-old Joseph and started running to Fort Wyoming, half a mile away. Ebenezer, lamed in a recent injury and unable to run, stood in the kitchen.

Two more Indians joined the slayer of Nathan Kingsley, and the three stood laughing at little Mary as she scurried toward the fort with her baby brother. Then they entered the house and a short time later emerged loaded with booty, carrying Frances and dragging Ebenezer and young Kingsley along. Mrs. Slocum, leaving her baby in the swamp, came to the Indians and begged on her knees for the return of the children. Noticing Ebenezer's lameness, the Indians contemptuously pushed him toward her, but shouldered Frances and the Kingsley boy and fled into the woods. Riflemen were already approaching from Fort Wyoming, but the Indians, who were of the Miami tribe, made good their escape. Young Kingsley was never heard of again.

Following the capture of Frances, the Slocums moved to Fort Wyoming for safety, as did Isaac Tripp, Jonathan's father-in-law. They kept their livestock on their land, where they had gathered hay and fodder, and each morning they went out with a guard of soldiers to water and feed the cattle. On the morning of December 16, Jonathan, his son, William, and Isaac Tripp went out without their usual escort to do their chores. The impression was that the Indians had moved north. As they arrived at the farm, a dozen warriors leaped from concealment. The three ran, but Tripp, an old man, was soon overtaken, speared nine times, and scalped. Jonathan was brought down by a bullet, slain, and scalped. William, though wounded in the leg, managed to reach the fort.

Ebenezer Slocum got over his lameness in time and, like his father, became a blacksmith and a farmer. He was also interested in military affairs and rose to the captaincy of the Wyoming Blues, the Wilkes-Barre company of the Pennsylvania Militia.

Ebenezer, an ambitious and enterprising man, formed a partnership with James Duane in 1798 and purchased land alongside Roaring Brook, near its junction with the Lackawanna River. This was in the township of Providence or, as it was sometimes called, Capouse or Capoose. Here the partners built a gristmill, the location being first known as Deep Hollow. Business was good. The gristmill was enlarged, a blacksmith shop was added, then a whiskey distillery and a sawmill. Ebenezer Slocum bought out his partner, Duane, and took his brother, Benjamin, into the expanding business, whereupon they erected a forge with two fires and a trip hammer. In a few years they were making most of the agricultural implements used by the farmers of the Wyoming and Lackawanna valleys. The two Slocum families had moved into the hollow, as had most of their workmen. In 1804 Ebenezer persuaded the government to establish a post office, and the settlement was given the name of Unionville.

In 1805 Ebenezer built himself a "mansion," the first frame house in Unionville; it was torn down in 1875, at which time it was the oldest house in the city of Scranton. In 1811 the Slocum brothers had two gristmills and the largest distillery in the region. Although the post office retained the name of Unionville, the people roundabout preferred to call this beehive of industry Slocum's Hollow, as an improvement on Deep Hollow. When the new century had rounded out its first quarter, the Slocum brothers arrived at the conclusion that they had made enough money. They shut down their plants and dissolved their partnership. Benjamin retired to his farm at Tunkhannock. Ebenezer took up a systematic search for the little sister who had been stolen by the Miami Indians thirty-seven years before.

In the year 1807 Ruth Tripp Slocum, widow of the murdered Jonathan, had called her sons to what she knew was her deathbed.

"Do not," she whispered, "ever give up the search for Frances. I know she is alive."

For years her sons and daughters contributed time and money to the seemingly hopeless hunt. At various times Frances's brothers made long treks into Indian country, searching for a white woman among the various tribes. The abductors of the little girl were never identified as Miamis until Frances, at long last, told her story. In

1826 Joseph Slocum believed that he had at last found her in the wife of a chief of the Wyandottes. However, the woman, who had herself been kidnapped, remembered enough to realize after intensive questioning that she was not Frances Slocum.

In January, 1835, George Ewing of Logansport, Indiana, who carried on an extensive trading business with the Indians, made a journey on the Mississineva River, a tributary of the Wabash. As night fell, he made a landing at Deaf Man's Village, near Peru, Indiana, camp of the Miamis, and called at the home of Mac-on-a-quah, wealthy widow of a chief of the tribe and an old friend of Ewing. The trader was welcomed, provided with a bountiful supper. After he had finished his meal, his hostess ordered the fire replenished —which surprised Ewing, for the Indian custom was to retire after the last meal. Mac-on-a-quah motioned her guest to sit across the hearth from her. She talked at length about her crops and her cattle; she was, as it turned out, gathering courage for a confession.

"I have something on my mind," she said at last. (She was talking in the Miami tongue with which Ewing was thoroughly familiar.) "I am old and weak. (She was sixty-two, but looked at least ten years older.) I shall not live long and I must tell it. I cannot die in peace if I do not."

Sitting by her fireside, Frances Slocum then related the story of her life to the trader.

"There!" she said when she had finished. The dawn was coming up and the embers were flickering on the hearth. "Now I can die. You can never know how this has troubled me." *

The only clues to her real identity with which Mac-on-a-quah was able to furnish Ewing were that she had been taken away from her father's house on or near the Susquehanna River when she was between five and eight years old. She believed that her family's name was Slocum; that her father was a Quaker, a small man who wore a large-brimmed hat; that he was sandy-haired and very freckled.

Ewing wrote a letter to the postmaster at Lancaster, Pennsylvania, knowing that to be an old and important town near the Susquehanna. The letter carrying Mac-on-a-quah's story was received by

* HARVEY, OSCAR JEWELL, *History of Wilkes-Barre,* privately printed.

Mrs. Mary Dickson, who, in addition to being the postmistress, was also owner and editor of the Lancaster *Intelligencer*. We can only hope that Mrs. Dickson was a better postmistress than she was an editor, for she tossed the letter into a drawer and paid no further attention to it. About two years later she sold the *Intelligencer* to John W. Forney, later editor of the Philadelphia *Press*, then clerk to the national House of Representatives and finally secretary to the United States Senate.

An employee found Ewing's letter to Mrs. Dickson among the flotsam and jetsam of the editor's desk and handed it to Mr. Forney, who knew a good story when its elements were before him. He published the letter and requested that any reader who could furnish further details do so. The Reverend Samuel Bowman, rector of St. James's Church in Lancaster, who had been born a stone's throw from the Slocum homestead in Wilkes-Barre, knew the Frances Slocum legend and at once forwarded copies of the *Intelligencer* to her brothers and sisters.

Isaac Slocum was deputized by the family to visit Mac-on-a-quah at Deaf Man's Village. He entered the aged widow's home, stared at her, and exclaimed:

"Good God! Is this my sister?"

Whereupon he seized her left hand and saw upon the forefinger the long scar, caused by a blow from a hammer on an anvil, by which the family had always claimed it would be able to identify Frances Slocum!

Mac-on-a-quah had forgotten her first name; she could not speak a word of English; she had been brought up as a member of the Miami tribe and had married She-po-con-ah, its war chief, by whom she had two daughters, both married to Miamis. She was well-to-do, the owner of a farm and large herds of cattle. Her relatives came to visit her, begged her to return to her own people. When she refused, they asked her at least to pay them a visit.

"I cannot, I cannot!" she replied. "I am an old tree. I cannot move about. I was a sapling when they took me away. I should not be happy with my white relatives. I am glad to see them, but I cannot go. I have done."

The Slocums continued to visit their sister and aunt at frequent intervals, but were never able to make her change her mind about returning to them. In 1840 the Miamis were ordered, with other Indians, to move to the new reservations in Oklahoma, then Indian territory. She appealed to her brothers to use their influence in having the government permit her to remain on and in possession of her farm. Her plea was placed in the form of a resolution and was passed by both House and Senate.

Soon the old white-woman-turned-Indian found herself surrounded and pestered by white land-grabbers. She was confused and unhappy and, at her request, her nephew, George R. Slocum, son of Isaac, came to live with her and to manage her affairs. Upon her death, March 9, 1847, George Slocum became a Baptist missionary to his aunt's adopted people and converted the majority of them to Christianity.

3   *William Henry—*
Henry Drinker

WHEN Ebenezer and Benjamin Slocum decided in 1825 to retire from activity as local ironmasters, coal merchants, farm-implement manufacturers and whiskey distillers, their settlement fell into decay. Everyone seemed to know that there was plenty of anthracite coal around for the digging, and iron, too, but there was no market in the immediate neighborhood for coal or iron beyond the settlers' needs for fuel and for plows to break the ground. The rising markets to the east were inaccessible.

However, the Schuylkill coal and iron fields, south of the Wyoming and Lackawanna valleys, were doing well. Reading (a borough in 1783, incorporated as a city in 1847) was founded in 1748 by William Penn's sons, Thomas and Richard. It was the first of the American settlements in iron and coal regions to take advantage of the mineral resources nature had bestowed upon them. Most of the cannon supplied to the Continental Armies was made in Reading. Both anthracite and bituminous coal had been found in the locality and were being dug long before the Connecticut men made up their minds to claim northeastern Pennsylvania.

Obadiah Gore, son of one of the first Connecticut men to settle in the Wyoming Valley, first found and used anthracite in the Lackawanna Valley. A blacksmith by trade—a tremendous number of the Connecticut settlers seem to have followed this calling—Obadiah set up a forge in 1771, beside the place where he had previously spotted surface anthracite, and used what the settlers called "stone coal" in the heating of iron ore, which he also found close by. During the Revolutionary War men of the Gore family dug anthracite and floated cargoes of it down the Susquehanna River. It was landed near Harrisburg and was hauled from there to Carlisle, where Washington had established an arsenal and where the coal was used in the preparation of iron ore—not shipped from the valley—for the making of munitions.*

Philadelphia financiers, such as Robert Morris and Benjamin Rush, had eagerly bought up land in the Schuylkill Valley and a charter for a railroad (later the Philadelphia and Reading Railroad Company) had been granted as early as 1791, construction beginning in 1830.

But, in the first quarter of the nineteenth century, nobody seemed to be particularly interested in the Lackawanna and Wyoming valleys. The region had suffered fearfully from Indian raids, bloody Tory incursions during the Revolutionary War, the Wyoming Massacre, and the Pennamite wars between the men of Pennsylvania and the men of Connecticut. The valleys had a bad name; settlers shunned them and only the hardiest took a chance and dug in.

It was a wild region, sparsely populated, while the rest of Pennsylvania was fast being tamed, and future cities were springing up in scores. Henry Drinker, a former surveyor-general of the state, was beginning to think rather poorly of a family investment of 25,000 acres of wild land in the Lackawanna region, east of what is now Scranton and between Tobyhanna and Dunmore, purchased in 1789 following decision of Congress against the Connecticut Claim. The investment was comparatively small—about fifty cents

* The statement that anthracite coal was shipped over the Susquehanna River for the purpose of munitions manufacture for the Continental Army (from R. Dawson Hall, Engineer Editor of *Coal Age* and contributing editor to the *Encyclopaedia Britannica*) is somewhat at variance with the claim of the Delaware and Hudson Company in its publication *A Century of Progress*, 1925, that the Delaware and Hudson Canal was the first carrier to move anthracite from northeastern Pennsylvania over water to market. The Delaware and Hudson, the first railroad in the country, sprang from the minds of the pioneer brothers, William and Maurice Wurtz, of Philadelphia, who, failing to buy coal lands in the Scranton region, purchased other properties at Carbondale and Archbold. The Wurtz brothers projected the canal, which eventually joined the Delaware and Hudson rivers (Honesdale, Pennsylvania, to Kingston, New York) and the first "gravity" railroad at Carbondale —to connect the mines with the canal, thus opening the anthracite coal market in New York City and in New York Harbor in 1829.

an acre—but Mr. Drinker, a Philadelphia Quaker who had gathered in a fortune by building turnpikes, was a careful man and believed that money should work hard to bring in more money. He also believed in using other people's money in preference to his own.

In 1819 Mr. Drinker decided that his property should be opened up with one of his turnpikes, which he laid down from the Delaware Water Gap as far as Tobyhanna. Primarily he was interested in settlers to take up his acreage, rather than in coal and iron. His turnpike, a vast improvement on the old road hacked through the forest by the Connecticut men half a century before, did, indeed, bring in settlers. It also brought, on a personal tour of inspection, William Henry, Scotch-Irish Pennsylvanian and distinguished geologist.

Mr. Henry had known for a long time that the land in the vicinity of Slocum's Hollow was rich in coal and iron deposits. He also realized that the region had to have transport facilities in order to move the product to market. He had watched the methods of William and Maurice Wurtz, the Philadelphia brothers who had been hunting coal beds and who had sought options in the Slocum's Hollow region from the original settlers, the Abbotts, the Taylors, the Howes, the Slocums, the Albros, and the Recketsons. Mr. Henry was pleased when the settlers rejected the Wurtz offer, and he watched the brothers with added interest as they trailed further north to open the Carbondale field, to form the Delaware and Hudson Company, and to cut a road to the seaboard coal market by means of a canal between the Delaware and Hudson rivers.

Mr. Henry cultivated the friendship of the Slocum's Hollow settlers, but he said nothing about options—as yet. Henry Drinker's turnpike was a step in the right direction, but carting over an early nineteenth-century turnpike was no way to haul coal to metropolitan markets. However, the road was bringing settlers on to Drinker's Covington properties east of Providence (north Scranton).

The migration was also noted by Thomas Meredith, a surveyor and promoter who had been interested in several railroad projects in Pennsylvania but who, having started the ball rolling, seems to have been pushed out of each venture by the New York and Philadelphia financiers to whom he had sold the ideas.

Meredith wished to push a railroad from the practically untapped

coal lands of the Lackawanna Valley northward into the already
prosperous agricultural area of southern and western New York,
with its more than a million inhabitants, only 50 miles away from
Drinker's property and only 100 miles away from Ithaca, on Lake
Cayuga, over which boats could be sailed to the Mohawk River
(and later to the Erie Canal).*

Meredith went to Henry Drinker with his idea. His railroad was
to lead from the mouth of Ligett's Creek in Providence (north
Scranton) to Great Bend, alongside the Pennsylvania–New York
border and on the Susquehanna River. Drinker told Meredith to go
ahead with a survey and presumably bore the cost of this investigation. The road was projected as the Lackawannock and Susquehanna
Railroad, and Drinker sought unsuccessfully to interest New York
and Philadelphia capital. The success of the Erie Canal had made
the stock-purchasing people of the New World very canal-conscious
and very wary of this practically untried railroad method of transportation.

At the same time another railroad idea was either suggested to
Drinker or came to him of his own accord—a railroad from the
Delaware Water Gap to Wilkes-Barre. He applied for and secured
a charter for the Susquehanna and Delaware Canal and Railroad
Company, which was planned as a gravity railroad or canal and
would carry coal from his own lands to the Gap. Coal at this time
was worth nine dollars a ton in Philadelphia, and Drinker could buy
about as much coal land as he cared to in the lower Lackawanna
Valley at ten dollars an acre. All he had to do was to get the coal
to market, but the Delaware River would have had to be deepened
at points and canalized at others before coal arks could float to the
seaboard. Drinker estimated that he could build his railroad and cut
his waterway for $700,000. He spent several years trying to do so,
but was unable to persuade the money men.

William Henry, the geologist, was deeply interested in Henry
Drinker's plans. Although it was he who ultimately raised the money
which made possible the beginnings of the Delaware, Lackawanna
and Western Railroad, he did not, in the eighteen twenties and early
thirties, consider himself a promoter. He did want to see a railroad

* BOGEN, J. I., *History of the Anthracite Railroads,* The Macmillan Company,
New York.

go through Scranton and, if and when it did go through, he wanted it to pass along that part of present-day Scranton which in his day was Slocum's Hollow.

Surveyor Thomas Meredith's plan came to light again when a group of New York State and Pennsylvania citizens gathered together at a "railroad convention" held in Ithaca, May 11, 1831. Both the Pennsylvanians and the New Yorkers agreed to go home and act as missionaries for a railroad line from the Wyoming and Lackawanna coal fields to Owego, New York, via Great Bend, opening a through route to the New York waterways. The proposed line from the fields to Great Bend was according to Meredith's survey and was called Ligett's Gap Railroad.

Both Henry Drinker and William Henry were present at the Ithaca meeting, where the former promised to make the journey to New York and there stir up interest in the project of the Ligett's Gap Railroad. However, when Drinker arrived in New York, the single project on which he had his instructions from the Ithaca convention had developed in his own mind into two. Along with the Ligett's Gap promotion, for which he sought $500,000 of capitalization, he also brought up the matter of his charter for the Susquehanna and Delaware Railroad, for which he asked that books be opened for subscription up to $1,000,000 of capital stock. The two roads, as Drinker explained it, were to form a continuous line from the Delaware Water Gap through the Lackawanna Valley to the New York state line just above Great Bend—the route later built by George Scranton and substantially followed today by a portion of the Delaware, Lackawanna and Western Railroad.

While Drinker was spreading his eloquence before the New York money men, William Henry took a trip to Slocum's Hollow, where, because of his earlier cultivation of the friendship of the settlers, he was able to take options on 503 acres of land, all of which is today within the boundaries of the city of Scranton. He was also able to renew these options from time to time as the railroad plans warmed and cooled, over and over again. Books had been opened for both of the Drinker projects, but very little money came in—not even enough to put on a show of beginning work.

In 1833 Henry Drinker had a third railroad dream, that of a gravity line along the Susquehanna from Pittston to the New York state line, to be called the Susquehanna Railroad. It should be remembered that in these very early days of railroading Drinker, his associates, surveyors, and engineers had no intention of running passenger railroads; they were interested only in freight, to be moved by horsepower or stationary engines and inclined planes. The panic of 1835–1837 seemed to call a halt on Drinker's three railroad projects—Ligett's Gap, the Susquehanna and Delaware, and the Susquehanna.

But slap in the middle of the panic there appeared an angel—in the eyes of ebullient Henry Drinker and cautious, option-picking William Henry. This was Lord Charles Augustus Murray, son and heir of the Earl of Dunmore and a kinsman, albeit very distant, of Victoria, Queen of England. Lord Charles, a pleasant, democratic soul, was also somewhat of a scapegrace and a trial and tribulation to his aristocratic relations. Rumor had it that he had been sent to America to cure him of a love for—and a possible misalliance with —"a young woman of the lower classes."

Genial, elbow-bending Lord Charles met Henry Drinker in Philadelphia at a gathering which was the equivalent in those days for what we now call a cocktail party. Drinker was aware that the young Englishman's family owned coal lands and that his father was interested in the beginnings of British railroads; what Drinker did not know was that the Earl of Dunmore's opinion of his son's business ability and financial acumen was something considerably below par. The young nobleman and the turnpike builder who also wanted to be a railroad builder became friends in a hurry. Drinker invited Lord Charles to inspect the proposed routes of his railroads and the almost virgin coal lands for which they were to be carriers.

Lord Charles knew nothing about coal mining or railroads; but he did know coal when he saw it, and here he was walking on it and kicking chunks aside, while he knew that, at home, men had to go underground to get it. He was more than enthusiastic. How much did his American friend need to get this black gold to market? Perhaps the young man well knew his family's opinion of him as a happy-go-lucky wastrel. Well, he would show them! There seemed to be as much coal here in the Lackawanna Valley as there was in all England. And in that conclusion he was absolutely right, though, in so far as he was concerned, it was just enthusiastic guesswork, inspired by a master salesman.

Mr. Drinker told Lord Charles that he could get the Susquehanna

Railroad job going comfortably for about $500,000 (then the equivalent in English money of about 100,000 pounds).

Meantime, and despite hard times, William Henry had managed to interest Edward Armstrong, a New York capitalist, in his options on the Slocum's Hollow lands. Mr. Armstrong's interest developed sufficiently for him to pay a visit of inspection to the Hollow just at the time that Lord Charles Murray was being feted by Henry Drinker, following the former's promise that the needed cash would be sent along as soon as he returned to the old country.

Happily for Mr. Henry, as it seemed at the time, Mr. Armstrong was pleased with the iron and coal possibilities, and he took up the options. The sales price of the Hollow was $8,000, and Mr. Armstrong paid down $500 as earnest money, having been called to New York by the sudden illness of a daughter. The deed was placed in trust until his promised return. He had previously made the acquaintance of Lord Charles Murray and of Henry Drinker. The latter named a townsite Dunmore after his friend's father, possibly with the idea that this honor might soften up the Earl for the coming half-million-dollar touch. William Henry was an incorporator on all three of Drinker's contemplated roads, and Armstrong was welcomed into the fold both as a landowner and as a probable source of ready money.

Everything looked rosy, despite the panic, when, out of the blue, things collapsed for William Henry. It should be explained here that he never had been able to make himself financially independent. One of the outstanding geologists, as well as surveyors, of his time, he had founded fortunes for others, but had never been able to accumulate one for himself. His faith in Slocum's Hollow and its mineral wealth had never wavered. Could he have bought the Hollow for the few thousand dollars which were but drops in the bucket for Edward Armstrong, he would have done so long before. But he did manage to secure option after option from his farmer friends. Now, in the development of the coal and iron field, he was to be a partner of Armstrong with whose help he felt that a Drinker railroad could be brought to pass through the Hollow.

Edward Armstrong arrived at his home in Orange County, New York, to find his daughter out of danger. A couple of days later he went riding, was thrown by his horse and killed. William Henry hurried to the Armstrong home and asked the widow and the children if they would complete the transaction by paying the balance of $7,500 due. The heirs refused, but admitted forfeiture of the $500. Henry went to the farmers, William Merrifield, William Recketson, and Zeno Albro. He had failed, through no fault of his own, but the earnest money now belonged to the holders of the land. Would they grant him a new option? The farmers slapped Henry on the back and told him not to worry.

From the Hollow the geologist went to visit Drinker, whom he found in a pleasant state of suspended animation, awaiting word of the arrival in Philadelphia of Lord Charles Murray's draft for $500,000.

"It would make very little difference to the original survey," observed William Henry as he sipped his drink, "if the line were to run through Slocum's Hollow."

"It would make a hell of a difference, Will," replied Mr. Drinker, who had not as yet learned of the death of Edward Armstrong. "I have some coal lands of my own, and that's where the road is going to run. But you won't be far away."

Before Henry could enter into further discussion, a mud-spattered horseman jumped to the ground by the porch of Drinker's home, ascended the steps, and whanged his riding crop on the door. A moment later a servant handed Drinker an envelope bearing the imprint of The Bank of Stephen Girard of Philadelphia. The bank's cashier was "honored" to enclose a communication from the Earl of Dunmore to the general effect that he had no intention whatsoever of investing any assets of the Murray family in any American railroad or coal-mine possibilities.

Henry Drinker was a good loser. He folded the communication, placed it on the mantel, turned to his guest.

"Lord Charles Murray," he observed quietly, "is not going to be able to help us. But for the cost of filing the papers, I would give Dunmore township another name. What about your friend, Edward Armstrong? Think he'd be interested in the railroad?"

"Mr. Armstrong," replied William Henry, just as quietly, "is dead. And his family has refused to complete the purchase of Slocum's Hollow."

4 *The Scrantons Bow In*

In the meantime, George and Selden Scranton were about to acquire the business which would lead to their eventual interest in railroads—the Lackawanna, in particular. This is how the Oxford Furnace came into their possession:

Jonathan Robeson of Philadelphia, born in that city in 1700, had been apprenticed when twelve years old to what was at that time a flourishing industry in colonial America, the manufacture of iron fireplaces and fireside equipment. At the age of twenty-five he was in business for himself, and fifteen years later, possessed of some means, he was looking for new fields to conquer.

The colonies were engaged in sporadic wars with French soldiers and settlers and almost continuous wars with the Indians. Jonathan Robeson saw a great future in the manufacture of cannon balls—not, of course, realizing the tremendous future in cannon balls to be evidenced in the War of the Revolution and in the Civil War. He sought a place in the country handy to iron deposits, forests, and charcoal. After a journey up the Delaware, he selected some acreage half a dozen miles east of the river, in New Jersey, and between the Beaver and Pohatcong rivers. Robeson persuaded a dozen of his Philadelphia foundrymen to accompany him, with their families, on this new venture.

The iron men arrived at their intended place of operation in the spring of 1741. First they cleared the land and built their cabins; then they went to work on the erection of a furnace. Robeson made his first cast on March 9, 1743. The settlement had been christened

Oxford and for 143 years, until the furnace fires were drawn for the last time in September of 1884, the Oxford Furnace (far later, the Warren Foundry and Pipe Corporation) was known throughout colonial America and then through the expanding United States as a premier manufacturer of fine cast-iron firebacks and fireplace equipment, nails, and iron pipe. Washington placed faith in the Oxford Furnace cannon balls during the Revolution, and Grant swore by them and never at them during the Civil War.

In his initial venture at Oxford Jonathan Robeson had interested two members of Philadelphia's famous Shippen family, Joseph and his brother, Doctor William. Gradually, after Robeson's retirement, the Shippens came into entire possession of the furnace and of the mansion house, erected nearby in 1754 by Jonathan Robeson for his son Maurice on the occasion of the latter's marriage. Maurice seems to have preferred Philadelphia to Oxford.

In 1809 Dr. William Shippen, Jr., then owner of the furnace and the mansion, offered them for sale. There was no immediate market for cannon balls, and brass and copper fireside furnishings were taking the place of those of iron. Another Maurice Robeson, son of Maurice the dilettante and grandson of the ironworks founder, put up what was left of the family fortune for the purchase of what had been the family business.

This Maurice Robeson seems to have had fair success in the manufacture of farm implements, sorely needed by the settlers of New Jersey as well as those of Pennsylvania. He operated the Oxford Furnace for thirty years, and at the mansion his son, George M. Robeson, was born, who was later to be Secretary of the Navy and a member of President Grant's cabinet for eight years. Maurice Robeson died in 1838, and a year later his widow and children sold the furnace and the mansion to George and Selden Scranton.

George Whitfield Scranton, the "father" of the Delaware, Lackawanna and Western Railroad, was born in Madison, Connecticut, May 23, 1811, and died in Scranton, Pennsylvania, the city he virtually founded, on March 24, 1861, two weeks before the start of the Civil War. He was a descendant of John Scranton, who had emigrated from England and settled in Guilford, Connecticut, in 1639. There is no record of the name of Scranton among any of the various pioneering and settling groups of Connecticut men in the region which the city of Scranton was later to dominate. The father of George and Selden Scranton was Theophilus, who operated a stage line between Saybrook and New Haven. As children, both Scranton brothers learned to groom and curry horses, to ride and to drive them.

Despite the fact that Theophilus Scranton made his sons work hard, in the early American fashion, he saw to it that they had the best education possible to his limited means. Both boys worked in their father's stables from early morning until it was time to attend common school. Lessons finished, they returned to their chores at the stables, and most of their evenings were devoted to study under the watchful eyes of their mother, Elizabeth, a former schoolteacher. In their teens, George and Selden attended Lee's Private Academy in Madison.

In 1828, when he was seventeen years old, George Scranton went to live with an uncle in the village of Belvidere, a couple of miles from Oxford Furnace. The reason for this change was an opportunity promised by his uncle for George to enter the general store operated by James Blair, a brother of John I. Blair (later to become one of the most famous of American railroad pioneers). The Blairs, a prodigious family of Scottish extraction, had already made a name for themselves as store operators in western New Jersey and northeastern Pennsylvania. An apprenticeship to a Blair in the mercantile field of those times was equivalent to an offer nowadays, under favorable auspices, to climb the ladder in Wanamaker's or Marshall Field's.

But when George Scranton arrived in Belvidere, the promised clerkship was not ready for him, and for three months he worked as a teamster. Behind the counter at last, he quickly impressed his employer with his affability, his salesmanship, and his sound knowledge of figures. What was more important, in so far as his future was concerned, George Scranton came to be known and appreciated by John Blair, who paid frequent visits to his brother. John at the time was operating the largest store of the loosely knit family chain at Gravel Hill, some ten miles due east of Delaware Water Gap. (As John Blair progressed in the world of business, finance, and railroad building, the name of Gravel Hill was changed to Blairstown.)

Legend has it—although there is no documentary evidence on the matter—that John Blair, still in his twenties, offered George Scranton the managership of his Gravel Hill store and that, in order to keep him at his side, James Blair was constrained to give the youth a partnership in his business. The story sounds like John Blair, who came to be ever on the lookout for likely young men to shape into railroad or bank presidents—and without compunction as to hiring them away from his friends. Whether it is true or not, James Blair did admit young Scranton into partnership before he had reached his twenty-fourth birthday. In 1835 George married Jane Hiles, daughter of a prosperous Belvidere farmer, sold his interest in the James Blair store, and took up the cultivation of land. Towns were springing up all around, and George Scranton saw a future in farm produce under sound business methods. He prospered.

Selden Scranton, like his brother, had taken up a store clerkship, first in Madison, Connecticut, and then in Philadelphia; from this he went to an iron foundry, rising from bookkeeper to manager. Thus employed, he made the acquaintance of William Henry, the geologist. Henry came to like the young iron founder, who was among the few who really listened to him, although it may have been that Selden Scranton's interest in possible Lackawanna coal and iron deposits was secondary to his interest in Henry's pretty daughter, Mary. In 1837 they were married, and a year later Selden Scranton was told that Maurice Robeson's widow would like to sell Oxford Furnace.

For a long time Selden Scranton had had his mind on the pressing need of this rapidly developing country for nails—plain, ordinary nails. Nobody seemed to be making these necessary adjuncts to home, village, and city building in the mass quantities that were required. True, there were factories in Boston and in New York, and some blacksmiths were willing to whack off a few thousand heavy, clumsy nails on order, but would rather make horseshoes and spades.

The Oxford Furnace, Selden Scranton considered, had lately deteriorated because of the handiness of purely local markets for rough farm implements. Every blacksmith was a toolmaker. If he could get hold of the place, he would turn out bar iron, make nails out of bar iron, and ship them everywhere. Widow Robeson wanted

$10,000 for the furnace and the mansion with its three-foot-thick walls. There was no use going to his father-in-law, William Henry, whose pockets were always as empty of cash as his head was full of ideas for lining those pockets.

Perhaps, thought Selden Scranton, Brother George has $10,000; or, perhaps George's father-in-law has; or, perhaps George could borrow. Anyhow, he got on his horse and was off to Belvidere.

George Scranton proved easy to convince as to the future of nails, and he could raise the money by the sale of his landholdings.

"There's another thing, Selden," observed George Scranton as they shook hands on the deal. "Talking of nails reminds me of rails."

"What rails?" asked Selden.

"Rails for railroads," replied George. "Railroads are the coming things in this country. Got it all over canals. And we're getting our rails from England."

"You've got to have iron and coal adjacent to each other for that," said Selden, "and in tremendous quantities. My wife's father claims the Lackawanna Valley's full of both. Cost too much to start up, and that hard coal won't smelt. And then, if you did succeed in smelting, like Jesse Fell claims to have done, how would we get the rails to a market that's all seaboard? England can ship quicker and cheaper than we can haul."

"For the present," replied George Scranton, "let it go. But while making nails, let's not forget rails."

5   *William Henry*
Takes Advice

WILLIAM Henry rode slowly down the dirt lane which was the main and only street of the Susquehanna County village of Abington Center. His horse was tired, for the two of them had come a long way from Henry Drinker's home.

The old geologist was as tired and dejected as his horse. One minute the railroad had been as good as there—to haul the coal and iron to market; the next minute—after his interview with Drinker —it was gone!

"Listen, Will!" Henry Drinker had shouted from his porch as his guest raised foot to stirrup. "Go see Andy Bedford. After all, he's got the railroad charter. Maybe, from what I hear, he can get his hands on some money."

True, Dr. Andrew Bedford had the Ligett's Gap Railroad charter. He had footed the bill for preliminaries back in 1832 after some smooth and convincing talk from Henry Drinker, who never laid out a penny if he could find someone else to do it. Bedford had renewed the charter again in 1837, when it had been in danger of lapsing, and was to do so again in 1842 and in 1847.

The old geologist came upon Dr. Bedford hammering together the boards of an addition to his cabin. He was a tall, lean, dark, bearded man—not unlike a future wartime President of the United States by the name of Abraham Lincoln—a middle-aged, horseback doctor whose practice extended from Glenwood to Slocum's Hollow and from Factoryville to Greenfield, 200 square miles of scattered settlements in forests and in valleys, on hills and by riversides. No wonder Dr. Bedford dreamed of a railroad—not so much to ease his own burden as to bring sick people within reach of medical aid and to entice more doctors to the Lackawanna Valley.

"Ah, there, Will," shouted Dr. Bedford, as he turned his head momentarily from his carpentering job. "Sit down and rest yourself. I'll be through in a few minutes."

Henry led his tired horse to the green grass strip behind the cabin and removed the saddle and bridle. As he sat down to wait for Dr. Bedford to be through, he noticed the scrawled black lettering on the doctor's nail barrel:

"Scranton Brothers. Oxford Furnace. New Jersey."

Nails, eh, thought William Henry as he filled his pipe. It was over a year since he had seen his daughter and her husband; not since Selden and George Scranton had entered into partnership at the old Oxford Furnace. He remembered that his son-in-law had said they were going into nails in a big way. Well, he ought to ride down into New Jersey and pay Mary a visit.

"How are those nails, Andy?" he shouted over the noise of the hammering.

"Best in America," grinned the doctor as he turned around and threw his hammer onto a small workbench. "One of those Scranton boys is your son-in-law, isn't he? I want to tell you, Will, they're really doing a business. Everywhere I go I see these Scranton nails."

They walked together into Dr. Bedford's combination bedroom, parlor, reception room, and office, and sprawled in homemade easy chairs. Dr. Bedford listened in silence as William Henry told his unhappy story.

"As far as I am concerned," the doctor said slowly, "I'll renew the charter of the Ligett's Gap Railroad every five years till kingdom come. Some day these valleys are going to be filled with people. But it doesn't look like that right now, does it, Will?"

Henry agreed that it did not. "But if I can get 'em started on the coal and iron in Slocum's Hollow . . . "

"*If* you can get 'em started," echoed the doctor. "Now I'll tell you something. I was at the Ithaca convention where Henry Drinker spread out all his plans. So were you. Then he went down to New

York and Philadelphia and talked to the money men. A railroad, Henry told them, would develop the country. He didn't get the money, but some day it will come. . . . Say, did Henry Drinker send you up here?"

William Henry admitted that he was in Abington Center at Mr. Drinker's suggestion.

"I thought so," said the country doctor, laughing loudly. "Sly old fox. He thinks I've got lots of money. Heard that uncle of mine who was a professor at Yale and put me through school there died a while back and left me a packet."

"Is it true?" asked William Henry, hardly able to keep renewed hope out of his voice.

"Fiddlesticks!" replied the doctor. "Uncle Amos did leave me all he had, a little over $2,000. I put it into land right around here. Coal land, too, if I don't miss my guess. I'm near enough to the Wurtz brothers and their Delaware and Hudson Company to sit quiet and wait."

"They made their market," observed William Henry.

"Yes," agreed the doctor. "The Wurtz boys have courage and money. They dug their coal close to the Delaware River, and then they cut a canal to the Hudson—and there was their market, down the river to New York."

Dr. Bedford knocked the ashes from his pipe, refilled and lit it.

"In New York and Philadelphia, when Henry Drinker was doing his spellbinding," he continued, "the man was selling a railroad. He talked of rich farming land, of the growth of towns, of easy communication with the lakes and the million inhabitants over the proposed route in New York State. And up jumps a little man by the name of Phelps, Anson G. Phelps, a big money man. And this Phelps snaps at Henry:

" 'What have you got up there besides potatoes and lumber?'

"Well, that phased Henry Drinker for a minute. But he comes back:

" 'We have coal, Mr. Phelps. The Wurtz brothers have proved that.'

" 'Yes,' says Phelps, 'and they've cornered the market with their railroad and their canal.' "

"I've got coal *and* iron," whispered William Henry.

"That's just what I'm coming to," replied Dr. Bedford. "Here's something about promoting money from people like Anson Phelps. You can't get, say, three-quarters of a million out of them to build a railroad through farmland and villages and forest. You won't get Anson Phelps to put money in schemes and hopes of that sort. But . . ."

"But what?" asked William Henry.

"Just this. You tell me you have an option on that Slocum's Hollow land. You know there's coal and iron there. I know it myself. Don't put the cart before the horse, Will. Buy up the property."

"But I haven't any money," objected the old geologist.

"No," admitted the doctor, "but your daughter's husband and his brother have. The Scrantons have been making money hand over fist since they went in the nail business. If they haven't what you need in cash, their name is good for it in any Philadelphia bank. Get them to put in a blast furnace. Selden Scranton is one of the best foundrymen in this country and his brother, George, is as smart a businessman as they come. The market is hungry for iron, and you'll have a sound argument for Anson Phelps and his kind when you go to them to ask for a railroad."

William Henry, his eyes alight, rose from his chair.

"I'll get going," he said.

"No hurry," said the doctor. "You have your option, the Scrantons have their starting money, or they can get it, and Phelps keeps his bank doors locked. There's a trundle bed here, so we'll sup and you can rest the night through."

"Thanks," said William Henry. "I'll be off to Oxford Furnace in the morning. And if anything comes of it, Andy, you're one of us."

"I have the railroad charter, Will," observed Dr. Bedford with a dry smile. "And when you're talking to the Scrantons, don't forget to mention those other railroads that are coming."

"Why?" asked William Henry.

"Because they'll need rails. American foundry-made rails."

6 *Iron into Steel*

As William Henry jogged along the trail toward Oxford Furnace, he thought about his options in Slocum's Hollow. Although he had secured an extension for sixty days and felt that if he needed more time he would get it, there was always the danger that others with money at their command would investigate and decide—as he had decided—that Slocum's Hollow stood in inadequate guard over a veritable treasure house. If cash were offered on expiration of his option, the farmers might be disinclined to renew with Henry.

Four weeks and four days had passed since the option had been renewed; he now had less than a month in which to take it up. It might be politic to visit around Slocum's Hollow before he rode on to Oxford Furnace.

So he halted his horse at the cabin door of Zeno Albro, one of the farmer-owners of the tract of 503 acres which Henry had surveyed and studied as to mineral content twenty years before. It should be made clear that the tract had little farming value. It was a bare strip of hard, black land, its below-ground treasure merely indicated by patches of surface hard coal. On this August day of 1840 William Henry, from Zeno Albro's door, could glimpse between the forks of the Lackawanna River and Roaring Brook the ruins of the sawmill, the gristmill, the distillery, and the furnace from which Ebenezer and Benjamin Slocum had reaped modest fortunes and which they had abandoned more than fifteen years before. It was wild land now, the portion cleared by the Slocums covered with a scrub growth of pine, oak, and hemlock.

Zeno Albro, interested only in crops and the clearing of land for more crops, and not at all in coal or iron, had news for William Henry—disquieting news. About three weeks before—some days after the Armstrong family had dropped their option—a party of three men had camped on the strip. Two of them rode horseback, while the third drove a wagon, loaded, according to Albro, with a tent, food supplies, surveying and other odd-appearing instruments.

Albro watched them carefully, he explained, but could learn nothing. Then one day they had a visitor.

"Know him?" asked William Henry, striving with poor success to be casual.

"Happen I do," grinned the farmer. "I get over into Jersey now and again. He's John Insley Blair, of Gravel Hill."

"John Blair!" repeated William Henry. "God Almighty! Zeno, I've got to be moving."

And move he did—fast. If John Blair was as pleased with his investigations of the Slocum's Hollow tract as Zeno Albro had reported, that option had to be taken up, and as speedily as possible. Eight thousand dollars, William Henry well knew, meant little to John Blair, but, at the same time, he would not put it out unless he was pretty certain of profit. At thirty-eight, John Insley Blair was already a power in the land. Not the oldest of the seven Blair brothers and the five Blair cousins, he was nevertheless the leader of that closely knit clan.

No use in taking the option to this hard-boiled titan, thought William Henry, as he galloped through the forest. No use at all in handing it over and asking to be declared in; undoubtedly John Blair knew all about William Henry's precarious circumstances and was well aware that all he had to do was wait—wait and pounce, with hard cash.

William Henry was an old man, but he spared neither himself nor his horse on his wild ride from Slocum's Hollow to Oxford Furnace.

Four men were sitting in the big dining room of the old Robeson mansion at Oxford Furnace. The August night was hot, but behind the three-foot-thick walls the men were comfortably cool. There was William Henry, rested and refreshed after his long ride, George and Selden Scranton, and their partner, Sanford Grant. The long table had been cleared of food and cloth to be replaced with bottles of port, glasses, pipes, and tobacco. The Scranton wives and children had retired.

"I have absolutely no compunction," George Scranton was saying, "about outwitting John Blair. No more compunction than he would have in outwitting us. And, mind you, this is no shady trick. Uncle Will, here, has been hanging onto that Slocum's Hollow option for years. He has come to us and he is entitled to our help." *

"But, George," observed Selden Scranton, "John Blair is our partner."

"I didn't know that," said William Henry.

"We needed nail cutters," explained Sanford Grant, "and we had a lot of bills receivable, mostly from Chicago, Cleveland, and Detroit. The banks would have loaned us money, but they wanted to be partners. They know a good thing when they see one. John Blair heard about it and he came along. After all, the Blair stores are our largest local customers. So we let him take up a fifth share."

"Maybe," said Selden Scranton, "we can let him in on the Slocum's Hollow deal—if we go through with it."

"Maybe," replied George Scranton with a smile. "Though I doubt if John would come in when he learns what is likely to happen. He would have to cool down, but he'll get over it in time. Now what about money, Sanford?"

"Can't very well take it out of the Oxford Furnace unless we declare John Blair in."

"Don't want to do that unless we have to; rather go to the banks. John's inclined to hog things . . ."

"Won't he be inclined to shut off our nail business with the Blair stores?" asked Selden.

* Only twice in his long, battling life was John Insley Blair outsmarted. The first time was when the Scranton brothers took up William Henry's option in 1840. His second defeat occurred thirty-nine years later, when Charles G. Wicker of the Dakota Southern Railroad Company cleverly blocked—on behalf of the Chicago and Milwaukee Railroad—Blair's almost completed grab of the Dakota on behalf of the Chicago and North Western System and turned it over to the Milwaukee. After that, John Blair, then seventy-seven, called it a day. (CASEY and DOUGLAS, *Pioneer Railroad*, McGraw-Hill Book Company, Inc., New York.)

"Not if I know John Blair," laughed George. "He's a partner. He's not going to take business away from himself."

"Well, if the Furnace is out of things, it boils down to what each of us has got. I could scrape up ten thousand . . ." said Sanford Grant.

"You were always better off than the rest of us," said Selden. "George and I have about fifteen thousand between us."

"Eight thousand for the property," mused George. "Say ten thousand for the furnace and preliminary operation—if we find everything as good as Uncle Will claims. Six thousand apiece. What do you say, Selden, Sanford?"

Both young men nodded their heads in agreement. Old William Henry, smiling happily, poured himself another glass of port.

"My report will stand up," he said, "and anthracite will smelt iron ore. The English have proved it now, and Ben Perry, over in Pottsville, has done it."

"What will we market?" asked Sanford Grant. "Besides raw pig? Nails, I guess?"

"And rails," replied George Scranton.

"Rails?" repeated Grant. Selden grinned at his brother.

"Railroad rails," said George. "England's in an iron slump. Thinks she's run out of ore. Maybe she has. There's more than thirty railroad charters between New York and Chicago where work is held up because they can't get strap rail from the old country. Where will they be when T rail is the thing?" *

William Henry had just a scant three days to go on his option when the Scranton brothers and Sanford Grant, who had brought two furnace experts and another geologist with them to Slocum's Hollow, decided that all was well and the deal was closed for the purchase of the property. Philip H. Mattes, owner of a tract in the Moosic Range three miles away, directed the attention of the new

* The superstructure of most railroads at the time George Scranton was dreaming of making T rail—solid rail—was composed of crossties, 9 feet long and 6 inches thick, which were laid 30 inches from center to center. On these were placed longitudinal rails of Norway or yellow pine, a portion 6 inches square and a portion 7 inches square, secured in place by triangular blocks or knees of scantling, firmly spiked to the ties on each side. Upon the longitudinal rails was an oak ribbon, 1¼ inches by 3 inches square, and on this ribbon an iron plate rail, 2½ inches by ¾ or ⅞ inches and weighing about 30 tons to the mile. This was strap rail. (CASEY and DOUGLAS, *Pioneer Railroad*, McGraw-Hill Book Company, Inc., New York.)

partners to the richness of the iron-ore veins on his land. He was invited into a partnership, shares being divided equally among William Henry, George and Selden Scranton, Sanford Grant, and Philip Mattes. The company was thereupon organized under the name of Scrantons, Grant, and Company. It is said that John Blair never mentioned to Henry or the Scrantons the matter of his own investigation and the possibility that he might have purchased Slocum's Hollow; neither did Henry nor the Scrantons ever mention it to Blair. Years before, when Blair had sought to have George Scranton manage his Gravel Hill store, he had evidenced his faith in the youth's ability and future. The Slocum's Hollow purchase was merely further proof for John Blair. In the years to come the two men were to be closely associated in various enterprises. To John Blair, George Scranton would have been a foeman worthy of his steel, but he preferred to have the younger man on his side.

The Egyptians are said to have made iron with hard coal five thousand years ago. Homer is authority for the Greeks' having done likewise three thousand years ago. The process was seemingly forgotten and reinvented time and time again. The modern record shows that iron was made with anthracite coal at Cardiff, Wales, in 1836, an achievement of deep interest to the United States.

In 1839 Benjamin Perry successfully smelted iron ore with anthracite at the Pioneer Furnace, owned by William Lymann, in Pottsville, Pennsylvania. Mr. Lymann was so impressed with the importance of his foreman's contribution to the future of the iron industry that he arranged to give a grand banquet in Philadelphia on July 4, 1840. It is significant that among the invited guests was John Insley Blair, who, a few days later, it will be remembered, despatched two geologists and a surveyor to study and report on the iron-ore and anthracite-coal possibilities in Slocum's Hollow.

It is also significant of the times—as well as an example of class distinctions inherited from England—that the horny-handed son of toil, Ben Perry, who had successfully "blown in" his furnace, was not numbered among the illustrious gathering which was to listen to Mr. Nicholas Biddle, of the Philadelphia Biddles, at that time president and principal stockholder of the Bank of the United States. Nevertheless, Mr. Biddle made a fine commentary on the importance of the achievement of the absent Ben Perry. A portion of it is worth repeating:

Let us see the changes which this simple discovery is destined to make. So long as the iron ores and the coal of the anthracite region were incapable of fusion, the ores were entirely useless and the coal nearly unavailable to the manufacturers. While, as the disappearance of the timber made charcoal very expensive, the iron of eastern Pennsylvania was comparatively small in quantity and high in price, and the defective communication with the interior made its transportation very costly.

The result was that, with all the materials for supplying iron in our own hands, our country has been obliged to pay enormous sums to England for this necessary article. In the two years 1836 and 1837 the importation of iron and steel amounted to upwards of twenty-four million dollars and the importations of the last five years have been about forty-nine million dollars. It is especially mortifying to see that even in Pennsylvania there have been introduced, within the last seven years, exclusive of hardware and cutlery, nearly eighty thousand tons of iron and that, of these, there were forty-nine thousand tons of railroad iron, costing in the neighborhood of three million five hundred thousand dollars.

Nay, in our visit to your mines, we saw, at the furthest depths of those subterranean passages, the very coal and iron brought to the mouth of the mines on rails of British-made iron sent to us from a distance of three thousand miles. This dependence is deplorable and it ought to cease forever.

The first Scranton furnace designed for anthracite took about eight months to erect. The job was superintended by William Henry, who was also busy laying out streets in Slocum's Hollow. He had succeeded in having the official post-office name of the growing settlement changed from Unionville to Harrison, in honor of William Henry Harrison, President of the United States, who had died not long before. George and Selden Scranton made frequent visits, but still had to give most of their time to the Oxford Furnace. Sanford Grant took up his residence in Harrison, kept the books, and ran a company store for the benefit of the workmen and the other arrivals who were already shaping the place into a town.

The first attempt to "blow in" was made September 4, 1841, almost a year to the day after the Scranton Company had taken over. It was a failure. Some changes were made in the furnace, and for a record of the gradual progress from failure to success we are indebted to the diary of Joseph C. Platt, an early employee of the Scrantons, their brother-in-law, and, later, one of their partners:

January 3 [1842]. Last night at about eleven o'clock the blast was put on the furnace under the superintendence of Mr. Henry, assisted by Mr. Clarke from Stanhope, New Jersey. At about three o'clock the furnace was bridged over the hearth.
January 4. Hiram and Henry Johnson and Radle are trying to work the furnace, but finding it too hard as the boshes above the temp were removed and the coal and ore let slide through.
January 6. Henry and Hiram and Williams digging salamander out of the furnace.

More failures. Selden Scranton made a hurried trip to Danville, where he had been told there lived a Welsh furnaceman, a recent immigrant, who claimed to have been one of those who had "blown in" the first anthracite-fired furnace in Cardiff. He found him in the person of John F. Davis, who, it turned out, had been telling the truth. Davis spent about a week making certain changes in the furnace construction, and Mr. Platt's diary began to sound more optimistic:

February 26. Blowing about two weeks without making any iron of consequence. After that the furnace began to work fairly. We blew out today in consequence of our heating oven being insufficient. Making iron—seventy-five tons, ten hundredweight.

So it could be done! Money was getting tight with the Scrantons and Grant; the job had taken longer and had cost more than they had figured. Therefore they did not feel like giving a banquet in Philadelphia with Mr. Nicholas Biddle in the chair.

In an undated memorandum, probably set down about the end of September, 1842, Mr. Platt wrote:

After putting in a new hearth and building two new heating ovens (under the direction of Davis, the Welsh immigrant), in addition to altering the old one, we commenced the last on the 23rd of May and continued until the 25th of September (eighteen weeks), when we were obliged to blow out in consequence of the blowing apparatus giving way, having been constructed too light in the beginning. Making 362 tons of iron, about 12 tons of castings.

Inside of six months, Mr. Platt was able to record a weekly average production of over twenty-seven tons:

After repairing bellows (wood-blowing cylinders), putting in new pistons, etc., we commenced the blast on the 11th of October (at five o'clock p.m.) and continued until the 12th of March, 1843 (twenty-two weeks). We were obliged to blow out for want of limestone. Making 583 tons, ten hundredweight of iron; castings about seventeen tons. Average per week 27 and 6/22 tons.

"We have now proved that we can make iron with hard coal," George Scranton told his partners. "The next thing we have to prove is that we can make a profit out of it."

Iron-ore deposits in Slocum's Hollow, while seemingly plentiful, called for considerable digging, and the partners turned to the Moosic tract, which Philip Mattes had contributed as his share of the venture. Since the deposits there were on top and almost pure, George Scranton decided to build his first railroad over the three miles between the furnace and the deposits. This was a rough-and-ready affair that operated by gravity. The wooden boxes on iron wheels ran on strap rails, rolling down on their own weight to the furnace and being horse-hauled back to the iron hole.

By July of 1843 the Scrantons were making an average of forty tons of iron a week. A relatively small portion of this was being turned into cut nails and being sold. John Blair could have had no complaint about splitting business, for the Oxford Furnace, in which he held an interest, was operating at capacity, even though the country was passing through one of its regular periods of depression. The swarm of railroad charters, on the implementation of which George Scranton had counted so heavily, were not producing orders for either strap rail or T rail.

Things did not look good, and both the Scrantons and Sanford Grant were shoveling all their Oxford Furnace profits into the hungry, blazing maw of the Harrison Furnace. What market there was for iron was on the eastern seaboard, and there were only two ways of getting the Scranton Company's product there. The first was by wagon to Carbondale, then by the Delaware and Hudson Canal Company's railroad to Honesdale, and thence by the canal from the Delaware to the Hudson River and on down to New

York. The second way was by wagon to Port Barnum (Pittston), a six-mile haul, and then by the North Branch Canal to Philadelphia, Havre-de-Grace, or Baltimore. The whole of the first year's product was disposed of in New York and Boston via Havre-de-Grace. But the market price of iron had dropped 40 per cent since the furnace had been put in proper shape by John Davis, and the Scrantons realized little more than the cost of transportation on their several shipments.

The brothers and their partners realized that one or more of several things had to be done: transportation costs had to be cut; the market had to go up or they would have to go out of business; they would have to open shops and manufacture more articles than nails from the crude iron. When George Scranton thought of other articles, his mind centered invariably on the manufacture of rails for railroads, but that possibility seemed further off then than at any time in the preceding decade. To put matters in a nutshell, the Scrantons had faith in the future, but they were running out of money with which to finance the present.

To a special meeting in William Henry's home in Harrison on September 3, 1843, were summoned two cousins of the Scranton brothers, Joseph H. and Edward C. Scranton, successful businessmen of Augusta, Georgia, who had previously expressed great interest in the ironworks. Present also were Philip Mattes, original owner of the Moosic ore tract; John Howland, a New York banker; Sanford Grant and William Henry. Mr. Henry, old and tired, resigned his partnership and was voted a small annuity, which, with the sale of his town lots, was to leave him in a very comfortable position for one of his simple needs.

The stock of the original company was increased from $18,000 to $86,000. George and Selden Scranton, along with Sanford Grant, were made working partners, drawing salaries in addition to their stockholdings; the others were stock subscribers and special partners. It was decided to build a rolling mill and, by making pig iron into bar iron and nails, to cut by 25 per cent the weight of the haul to market and at the same time to increase values with finished products. The depression was slow in shaking out, but the rolling mill was completed in late winter of 1845 and in April the first iron was puddled.

That summer George and Selden Scranton became permanent residents of the thriving settlement which was now being called Scrantonia (later Scranton). The post office was in Providence Township to the north. A year later Joseph H. Scranton moved in. The brothers bought out Sanford Grant's interest in the Harrison ironworks, but the latter apparently retained his holdings in the Oxford Furnace. Joseph C. Platt, the diarist already referred to, and the husband of Catherine, sister of George and Selden Scranton, was elevated to a working partnership, and the firm's name was changed to Scrantons-Platt Company. The rolling mill and the manufactured products were keeping the plant on an even keel and taking care of salaried executives and employees, but profits were not sufficient to pay dividends. George Scranton now began to experiment with the manufacture of T rail. The railroad-building business, after a long period of stagnation, appeared to him to be looking up.

7   *Rescue of the Erie*

WILLIAM Earle Dodge sat in his office on lower Broadway, New York, one fine spring morning of the year 1846, fingering a letter which had reached him by the special delivery methods of those days. Placed in charge of an English ship's captain at Plymouth, it had been brought by a member of the crew to the office of Phelps, Dodge and Company, financiers, copper, iron and wholesale dry-goods merchants, fifteen minutes after the ship had docked at the Battery.

It was indeed an urgent missive. The London iron factor who had penned it regretted to inform Mr. Dodge that he was unable to gather together for the New York and Erie Railroad Company a promised shipment of 12,000 tons of railroad T rails which Mr. Dodge, as purchasing agent of the Erie, had ordered for the laying down of its proposed Delaware division, to run from Port Jervis, New York, to Binghamton, passing through Susquehanna, Pennsylvania. The Londoner admitted that he had accepted this order in good faith and had been fighting to assemble the T rail for shipment.

It had not been his fault, he complained, that in ordering the material he had run slap into England's first great railroad expansion. Between 1845 and 1850 the little island, just a trifle more than 600 miles in length, and half that at its greatest width, jumped railroad construction from 2,235 miles to 6,635 miles. The British roads had secured priority on iron, and there was nothing the London factor could do about it. He could not get his hands on a single ton of rails—to say nothing of 12,000 tons.

This, mused Mr. Dodge, was a terrible state of affairs. Six months ago the New York State Legislature had passed a bill donating to the New York and Erie Railroad the sum of $3,000,000 for right-of-way purchase and construction. There was a condition to the gift. The Delaware division rails had to be laid within eighteen months. One third of the time had elapsed; instead of this letter, admitting inability to deliver, Mr. Dodge had been looking for the ship which would bring in the first installment of rails to be delivered at Port Jervis on the Delaware River.

With the letter in his hand, Mr. Dodge walked out of his office, through the great room occupied by the clerks and salesmen of Phelps, Dodge and Company, and so came to the sanctum of his father-in-law, Anson Greene Phelps, senior partner of the concern. Without a word he passed the letter to the grizzled little man behind the huge flat table which served him as a desk.

Anson Phelps read the letter slowly and looked up at his tall, handsome son-in-law. They were both directors of the Erie.

"Looks like we're going to forfeit that three million," observed Dodge.

"Looks like England is going to lose her T-rail business," rejoined Phelps. "We've been flummoxed, Will. So they're planning four thousand miles of new road; and so they keep their iron. Where are they going to get four thousand miles of line on that little rock? And after they get it down, if they do find places to put it, then they'll be willing to sell us rail again. I say to hell with them!"

"Anson!"—sharp rejoinder and definite rebuke.

"Sorry, Will," grinned the little old man. "I forgot." *

"Have you any suggestions?" asked Dodge.

"You bet your boots I have. I've got a solution, too, I think. Ever hear of those Scranton boys up in the Lackawanna Valley?"

"Nail makers, aren't they?"

"Yes, they're nail makers." Mr. Phelps was having difficulty in

* William E. Dodge, a deeply religious man, was the pioneer of temperance in the United States, both in language and in liquor. It was his money and his leadership which first made New York a prohibition state in 1854. Men seeking business or favors from him did well to curb their tongues, even in the mildest forms of cussing, when in his presence—a difficult job in those free and easy days.

keeping his language on the courtly level insisted upon by his son-in-law. "And good ones, too. But that's not all of it. I happen to know they've been experimenting with T rail for the last two or three years." (Benjamin Loder, President of the Erie, a friend of the Scrantons, had given Phelps this information.)

"That's a big order," observed Dodge. "Twelve thousand tons. Are they equipped for fast work? There's a time limit, you know."

"If they're not equipped," snapped Phelps, "we'll equip them. That is, if their stuff stands up. Take a run up there, look over their plant and, if you think they can handle the order, bring them down to me."

Two weeks later George and Selden Scranton sat in Anson Phelps's office on the other side of the fiery little man's huge table. Present also was William Dodge, whose report on the brothers had been favorable—especially since they had on hand about two thousand tons of T rail.

"That's a lot of rail," observed Anson Phelps, "particularly with no orders in sight."

"We had to keep working," replied George Scranton, "and we knew the market would be there eventually. We scrapped a lot of stuff, experimenting, before we got that stock pile. As Mr. Dodge has told you, it's good rail."

"Think you can fill the order?" asked Phelps. "That is, if you get it."

"We can start shipping at once over the Delaware and Hudson Canal and down the Hudson River and deliver along the right-of-way as the line is laid to Binghamton. We'll start building a second furnace right away."

"The price you gave Mr. Dodge," said Phelps, glancing at a memorandum, "was $46 a ton?"

"Delivered to the railhead as it moves," replied George Scranton.

Anson Phelps glanced at the memorandum. The London factor's price was $80 a ton, delivered across the Atlantic at Port Jervis.

"Get up a contract, Will," directed Phelps. "The last 500 tons to be on the right-of-way no later than four weeks before the state's deadline. Just a minute. Gentlemen, what about your financial responsibility? Able to carry out this deal C.O.D.?"

The brothers glanced at each other.

"You tell him, George," said Selden Scranton.

"I think," Anson Phelps interrupted with a smile, "you're going to tell me something I already know. But go ahead, George."

The use of his Christian name by the hard-headed financier made explanation a little easier. George Scranton came to the point at once.

"Mr. Phelps," he said, "we're flat broke. If we get this contract, which to us means the difference between continuing in business or closing up, we will have to get a lot of new machinery. We will have to build that second furnace. We can't take it on without an advance. But we have those two thousand tons of rail ready for delivery."

"You're in a bit of a fix, George. Well, if it comes to that, so are we. Quit making faces at me, Will Dodge. I guess these boys know all about the state's deal with the Erie. Two thousand tons of rail at $46 a ton; that makes $92,000. If I get you a check for $100,000 from the Erie Board, will that put you on your feet?"

"Handsomely!" chorused the brothers.

"Right. Will, have that contract ready to sign in the morning. I guess we can have your check ready for you, too. Dine with me tonight, both of you. Will, join us after dinner. I know you hate the sight of good liquor on the table, but I think that these gentlemen and I have earned a drink or two. Then, tomorrow, be off with you and get to work."

Those boys, thought Anson Phelps as the door closed, are worth watching.

Within a year from the signing of the T-rail contract with the Erie, the firm of Scrantons-Platt Company had added three more furnaces to their ironworks. They were making most of the T rails being used wherever railroads were being laid down and were working night and day to fill their orders. The tiny settlement of a hundred odd, through which William Henry had ridden so dispiritedly little more than half a decade before, now boasted a population of over 7,000; a large proportion of these were foreign-born—Irish, Scotch, Welsh, English, Germans, and Poles. Many of them had been coal miners or ironworkers in the old country, and they came naturally to the region which seemed to promise steady work in their own field at good wages.

In October, 1847, the capital of the company was increased to $250,000, and a number of new-found friends and well-wishers climbed aboard the Scrantons-Platt band wagon. Anson G. Phelps came along, as did William E. Dodge. Soon after their election to the board two handsome contracts bobbed up from the Erie: one for 8,000 tons of rails at $65 to $75 per ton; another soon afterward for the same amount of tonnage with prices from $75 to $85 per ton. Another notable who arrived on the board at this time was John Insley Blair, with his brother, James—the latter the man who had given George Scranton his general-store clerkship at Belvidere eighteen years before; also elected was Benjamin Loder, president of the Erie.

The Scrantons and their brother-in-law were now in fast company, but they were well aware of it and fully able to cope with these captains of industry who had come to sit at their board table. Maybe one or two of these captains would have had no hesitation in grabbing away what was now the biggest rail foundry in the country —to say nothing of the added assets of coal and iron deposits spread over 10,000 acres of company land. With weaker men it is more than likely that the plant and its acreage would have been gobbled up, as many new industries and businesses were gobbled up in those hard, ruthless days. But Phelps and Dodge—and particularly John I. Blair, who had reason to remember—had measured the Scrantons and had realized that they could not do without them; and the Scrantons, now that every railroad in the country was pleading for T rail, might very well be able to do without Phelps or Dodge or Blair.

George Scranton's first railroad venture has already been told— the building of three miles of "gravity" strap from the Moosic iron-ore mine to his furnace head. In tracing the development of the Delaware, Lackawanna and Western Railroad—in so far as Scranton, "the father of the line," is concerned—there might be several starting points. The Lackawanna is a road almost entirely made up of mergers, consolidations, and purchases; and George Scranton's construction of the Ligett's Gap Railroad—which became the Delaware and Lackawanna and then the Delaware, Lackawanna and Western—might be considered the cornerstone of the system. However, Scranton's purchase and reorganization of the Cayuga and Susquehanna Railroad, formerly the Ithaca and Owego, illustrates better the builder's thinking processes toward his goal.

The Ithaca and Owego, the oldest portion of the Delaware, Lackawanna and Western Railroad, is now known as the Ithaca Branch. It was the second railroad to be incorporated in the State of New York. The organizers wanted communication from the waters and the country of the north and the west with the Susquehanna River on the south—a short haul between the navigable waters of New York and Pennsylvania.

The Ithaca and Owego Railroad (Incorporated January 28, 1828)

The sum of $150,000 was subscribed and the charter was dated January 28, 1828. Chief among the incorporators was Simeon De-Witt, surveyor-general of the State of New York and owner of a large tract of land at the head of Cayuga Lake. Little was done, however, for a couple of years, until Mr. DeWitt was stirred into a frenzy of action by pending construction of the Chemung Canal, from the head of Seneca Lake to Elmira—definitely a threat to divert trade from Ithaca and Owego.

DeWitt resigned his state job and took over the building of the railroad. By the summer of 1832, he had completed the north end and sought and obtained a capital stock increase to $300,000. The line was completed April 1, 1834, and the stock was again increased, this time to $450,000. It was, of course, a strap road. It was horse-hauled until 1836, at which time DeWitt thought it advisable to buy one of those new-fangled railroad engines.

This engine was ordered from the shop of Walter McQueen of Albany. It was Mr. McQueen's first crack at building a railroad engine and, although history fails to clear up the matter, it is believed to have been his last. The monster had no official name, but was known around the countryside as "Old Puff." Its main bother was a chronic loosening of the joints, which allowed a lot of steam to escape, halting any attempt at a speed of more than an ordinary walk and making the approach of "Old Puff" in the distance something frequently mistaken for a cloudburst moving in slow motion. Its tank was a barrel mounted on a tender, preceded by another tender loaded with wood.

"Old Puff's" job was to haul out of Ithaca at seven in the morning, which it usually managed to do. It was scheduled to arrive at Owego (27 miles) at eleven. During its two years of service "Old Puff" hit the morning schedule three times, but it is only fair to state that on one run, right after a joint-resoldering operation, it was so rejuvenated that it landed in Owego ten minutes ahead of its time, and such was its spirit that it went clear through the depot building. The return journey was from Owego at five in the afternoon, arriving at Ithaca (supposedly) at nine.

James Merrill, an old-time Lackawanna despatcher at Scranton, and an employee in his youth of the Ithaca and Owego, left some notes on the conduct of "Old Puff," which, although three quarters of a century old, make pleasant reading. For example, the rear car of the train was a favorite gossip place with traveling horse traders. From their hands dangled halters, at the other ends of which were horses, not trotting but walking sedately behind and at the sides of the car.

According to Mr. Merrill, "Old Puff" gathered such a dawdling reputation that good walkers refused to buy tickets on the line, claiming that they could get to their destinations faster on their feet.

On one occasion a load of passengers heading out of Ithaca for a political meeting in Owego arrived there all right—but on foot, pushing "Old Puff" and the rest of the train ahead of them.

The public was thoroughly disgusted and so, it would appear, was "Old Puff"; one summer evening it went through a bridge and into a creek between Catatonk and Candor, killing the engine driver and completely wrecking the bridge. The engine was dragged out of the water and retired to a shed, and the Ithaca and Owego went back to being horse-hauled. Our historian, Mr. Merrill, secured the job of driver, and, by applying a sharp pointed stick to the nags' rumps, won the deserved nickname of "Express" Merrill.

But even the proddings of "Express" couldn't keep the road out of the red. Previous to his death, former Surveyor-General DeWitt had managed to get a state loan of $300,000 on the road and equipment. The state foreclosed when the line failed to meet two years' interest charges. On May 20, 1842, it was put up at auction and knocked down to Henry Yates and Archibald McIntyre for $18,000. The road was reorganized and rechristened the Cayuga and Susquehanna Railroad Company. With "Express" Merrill still at the "throttle" with his pointed stick, it continued a lackadaisical life until the fall of 1848, when it was purchased by George Scranton and William E. Dodge for $50,000. All they sought was the right-of-way.

The main object in purchasing the Cayuga and Susquehanna was to reach a more northern market for the product of the Scrantons-Platt anthracite coal fields, which they knew was also to be the chief source of revenue of the Ligett's Gap Railroad, the promotion and establishment of which was seething. George Scranton, who had now left the manufacture of T rails to his brother and brother-in-law, undertook to have the road in working order by Christmas of 1849, a feat that seemed impossible. But it was done.

The old strap rails were removed, and the track was relaid with Scranton T rail. At Owego the line was extended to connect with the Erie Railroad, and the track was made into a 6-foot gauge to conform. At Ithaca the location of the terminus was moved and a new one built. These improvements cost about $350,000 and were pushed with so much vigor—an engine named "Orange" being borrowed from the Erie Railroad Company for construction purposes

—that relays of workers, laying the rails even by moonlight, had the road ready for traffic by October of 1849.

The first train on the newly constructed line was run December 17, 1849, starting from Ithaca. The occasion was one of considerable rejoicing, and all passengers rode back and forth as guests of the road. The engine was the "G. W. Scranton." Before starting the train, it was found that there was not enough wood in the tender to take it to Owego, whereupon the bystanders helped to saw up some of the old Ithaca and Owego track ties, and soon the tender was filled to overflowing. Everybody from George Scranton down to "Express" Merrill enjoyed himself that day. As a coal carrier for Scrantons-Platt, the Cayuga and Susquehanna brought in a steady yearly profit, and on April 21, 1855, it was leased in perpetuity to the Delaware, Lackawanna and Western Railroad at an annual rental of $54,600. In its new form it was first called the Cayuga Division, but is now known as the Ithaca Branch.

8 *Birth of the Lackawanna*

FROM making rails to building railroads seems to have been just logical progress, in so far as George Scranton was concerned. In later years he had a favorite piece of advice for all railroad men:

"Keep your freight moving. But at the same time keep your freight yards full."

This was sound caution with respect to his own railroad; but those were prerefrigeration days, and while no harm would come to coal or to iron rails waiting to be delivered, Mr. Scranton's advice could not have applied, for example, to Eleazor Lord's New York and Erie Railroad, for a major part of this line's early business was the hauling of milk, butter, and eggs to the rapidly growing City of New York. Neither would it have applied to William Butler Ogden's Galena and Chicago Railroad, which was so completely farm-to-market that it eventually halted short of Galena's lead mines and was devoted solely at first to hauling wheat, corn, and potatoes for that other fast-rising city, Chicago.*

George Scranton was interested in carrying coal, rather than iron. He had built his steppingstone to fortune—and that of his brother and his brother-in-law—out of iron. Geologists had told him that iron was exhaustible in his valley, that coal seemed inexhaustible. Anthracite could smelt iron, and the product could be turned into iron highways which could—and would—span the nation, up and

* CASEY and DOUGLAS, *Pioneer Railroad*, McGraw-Hill Book Company, Inc., New York.

down, across and along. But digging coal was simpler and easier than puddling iron. The markets were there, all over this rapidly expanding nation; all that had to be done was to bring the market for coal near enough to the pit heads to make the commodity easily available to business, industry, and the home. There was only one answer—a railroad, or railroads.

In purchasing, reorganizing, and refurbishing the Cayuga and Susquehanna Railroad in the fall of 1848, George Scranton and his partner, William E. Dodge, acted as individuals, not so much to cloak the ultimate object in view as to conform with the New York State laws regarding "foreign corporations." Scrantons-Platt, in which both men were partners, could not have bought it. (The "foreign-corporations law" was soon a dead letter, as regarded carrier corporations.)

The Erie, as has been related, was already building its Delaware Division from Port Jervis to Binghamton with T rail supplied by Scrantons-Platt. From there the road continued to Dunkirk, on Lake Erie, with its low-cost water route to the growing cities, towns, and hamlets of the Great Lakes and adjacent territory. William E. Dodge was a director, as well as purchasing agent, of the Erie; his father-in-law, Anson G. Phelps, was also a director. Both these men were on the board of Scrantons-Platt; so was Benjamin Loder, president of the Erie in succession to Eleazor Lord.

Despite the close association of Dodge with the Erie, he, as an individual in partnership with George Scranton, bought the Cayuga and Susquehanna. A glance at the map shows the Cayuga and Susquehanna running from Owego to Ithaca, on the shore of Cayuga Lake. Already George Scranton, in his chosen future role of coal carrier, was in negotiation with Dr. Andrew Bedford of Abington Center and his associates, who were still holding grimly to the old, oft-renewed Ligett's Gap Railroad charter, for purchase and construction of the line from the Scranton coal fields to Great Bend, situated on the state line between Pennsylvania and New York.

The Erie, building from Port Jervis through Lackawaxen and along the Delaware River to Deposit, would, in the interests of the most easily graded route, have to dip into Pennsylvania at the bend of the Susquehanna at the village of Lanesboro (now the town of

Susquehanna) and come out at the village of Great Bend and so on into Binghamton.*

It seems definite that, before acquisition of the Ligett's Gap charter, an agreement had been made (which later was carried out) whereby that road, when it reached its northern terminus of Great Bend, would be accorded passage over the Erie tracks through Binghamton to Owego, the southern terminus of the Cayuga and Susquehanna, the individual property of George Scranton and William E. Dodge.

The ethics of Mr. Dodge, a director of the Erie, in purchasing a short line which—with a leasing arrangement over the Erie tracks—might be considered competition with his own road, could be open to question by some people. The facts are that George Scranton arranged the preliminaries of the purchase of the completely foundered Cayuga and Susquehanna from Henry Yates and Archibald McIntyre; needing ready cash to complete the deal, he called in William E. Dodge, who contributed his share, as an individual and not as a director of the Erie. Sometimes it is best, in retrospect, to look on such things from the bright side.

As for George Scranton, the coal carrier, his plan was crystal-clear: to build the Ligett's Gap road from Scranton to Great Bend, there connecting with the Erie and the western New York coal market; later on, a road to Buffalo and the Great Lakes trade and on to markets being carved out of the wilderness. To the southeast from Scranton he visioned the Delaware and Cobb's Gap line—another charter gathering mildew—to the eastern seaboard market. He was already working on the Cobb's Gap plan when he began to build the Ligett's Gap road.

Of the sixteen commissioners who arranged for the charter of the Ligett's Gap Railroad in 1832, only three appear to have been

---

* This was also in violation of the "foreign-corporations" law, loosely, it would seem, adhered to by the state of Pennsylvania as well as New York. According to the distinguished railroad authority, the late Edward Hungerford, at one time an employee of the Erie, the matter of the "trespass" into Pennsylvania was "arranged and approved" by the legislature, on agreement by the Erie to pay the state $10,000 a year. However, as Mr. Hungerford pointed out, the Erie was already "trespassing" without charge in Pike County, Pennsylvania, between Port Jervis and Lackawaxen. Apparently this permission was granted before Pennsylvania—or some Pennsylvanians—realized that the Erie was a soft touch. (HUNGERFORD, EDWARD, *Men of Erie,* Random House, New York.)

living or active when George Scranton put before Dr. Andrew
Bedford his proposal to activate the charter, incorporate, and open
books for subscription. Dr. Bedford, as has been told, had renewed
this charter at his own expense every five years since its inception.
Less sanguine, but retaining their hold on the powers of the document, with its privileges of right-of-way purchase and surrender,
were Henry Drinker, who had originally financed the Meredith
survey and a later survey by James Seymour, and Jeremiah Clark.
The three originators were promised blocks of stock.

At a meeting in Scranton on March 7, 1849, 5,026 shares of stock
were taken up at $50 for each share, a total of $251,300. At a
subsequent meeting, January 2, 1850, John J. Phelps, New York
financier and distant cousin of Anson G. Phelps, was elected president. Charles F. Mattes, son of that Philip Mattes who had been an
original partner of the Scrantons, became secretary, and Selden
Scranton was chosen treasurer. The directors had the Erie's agreement as to the use of its tracks. On March 27 there was a reshuffling
of officers. Selden Scranton wished to devote his entire time to coal
and iron production, and his place as treasurer was taken by Roswell
Sprague, of New York. Mattes, giving the same reason, was replaced
by Henry Hotchkiss, of New Haven. The Board of Managers—
here began the practice of the Delaware, Lackawanna and Western
Railroad in referring to its directors as managers—was composed of
John Howland and William E. Dodge, both directors of Scrantons-
Platt; Edward Mowry; Drake Mills; and Moses Scott (all New York
financiers or industrialists); and John B. Williams of Ithaca, a banker
and dock-builder. George Scranton was appointed general agent
and builder of the road.

Construction work was begun almost immediately. Mr. Scranton
appointed as his chief engineer Major Edwin McNeil, a veteran of
both the Philadelphia and Reading and the Baltimore and Ohio Railroads. His mechanical superintendent was David Dotterer of the
firm of Dotterer and Darling, engine builders of Reading; Mr.
Dotterer had built the machinery required in a hurry when the
Scranton brothers secured their first T-rail contract with the Erie.

In order to start hauling coal as quickly as possible, those sections
over the valleys were built of trestlework made of rough timber.
These trestles were gradually filled in with earth so as to form em-

bankments and were known as "fills." The principal trestles were at Factoryville and Humphrey's Hollows; and there was a lot of trestlework for the switch over the Tunkhannock Mountain, so that the road could be opened before the completion of the Tunkhannock Tunnel. The gauge was 6 feet, to conform with that of the Erie.

The territory presented serious physical obstacles. The worst grades were those as the road ran out of Scranton, just as the worst grades in the later construction of the Delaware and Cobb's Gap line were in getting out of that town. At first mules and horses were employed, but they were a lot of trouble, particularly at the trestles. George Scranton decided that he needed a locomotive or two, and his mind went back to that exasperating and wheezing contraption, "Old Puff," which had been left rusting in a Cayuga and Susquehanna shed after it had plunged into a creek, smashed a bridge, and killed its engineer.

"Old Puff" was placed on a raft at Owego, floated down the Susquehanna River to Pittston, and then hauled over the Pennsylvania Coal Company's gravity road to Scranton. Mechanical Superintendent Dotterer performed a couple of major operations on this hunk of iron and put it to hauling ties and rails, but it was balky as ever and was soon junked. However, its partial resuscitation gives it a certain claim to fame. It had been officially named "Pioneer" and was the first engine of the Ligett's Gap Railroad and therefore the first engine of the Delaware, Lackawanna and Western Railroad system.

On April 14, 1851, a supplement to the Ligett's Gap charter was approved by the state legislature, changing the corporate name to The Lackawanna and Western Railroad. Soon afterward, probably tiring of "Old Puff's" pranks, Mr. Dotterer bought the engine "Spitfire," a veteran of the Reading road; "Spitfire" did yeoman work. The day after he was appointed general agent of the road, Mr. Scranton ordered three freight engines from the firm of Rogers, Ketchum, and Grosvenor of Paterson, New Jersey. The first of these, "Lackawanna," was delivered June 10; the second, "Tunkhannock," on June 25; and the third, "Capouse," on September 13. These cost $10,500 each. The first two arrived in good time to help "Spitfire" on construction work. The original subscribers were called upon during the summer to take up a $900,000 issue of 7 per cent ten-year bonds for equipment of the road. Unlike the Erie, which always had trouble financing and refinancing, Scranton's enterprise could call for the cash from the moneyed men of New York whenever it was needed. The road's first three passenger engines, "Wyoming," "Montrose," and "Abington," were all on hand when the line opened. These were also built by Rogers, Ketchum, and Grosvenor and cost $7,800 each.

The Ligett's Gap Railroad (Incorporated April 7, 1832). Genesis of the Lackawanna

A short description of the Ligett's Gap Railroad, as originally laid, deserves a place here. Starting from Scranton, 740 feet above tidewater, the line crossed the Lackawanna River and ascended the Tunkhannock Mountain on an average grade of 75 feet to the mile. About two miles from Scranton was Ligett's Gap, locally known as "The Notch." The ascent continued to Clark's Summit, seven miles from Scranton and 502 feet above that station. Here there was a wood station and a spring of water before a tank was put in. Some really fast running came to be done on this grade down to Scranton when enginemen were late for supper. From Clark's Summit the grade fell at the rate of about 62 feet per mile to the south branch of the Tunkhannock River. The road then ascended a ridge called Ark Swamp, stretching between the main Tunkhannock and its south branch. This ascent averaged 20 feet to the mile and the summit was passed by the Tunkhannock Tunnel, 2,250 feet long, a work of magnitude and well constructed. On leaving the tunnel, the grade descended to the Tunkhannock River, which it crossed at an elevation of 78 feet.

From this point, the line followed Martin's Creek Valley for about 19 miles until it reached New Milford summit, 418 feet above Scranton, the grades being about 21 feet per mile. From here the road descended about 35 feet per mile to the Susquehanna River, which it (originally) crossed by a Howe truss bridge 600 feet long in order to connect with the New York and Erie Railroad at Great Bend, 53½ miles from Scranton. This is the line, as originally built, and some deviations have since been made. The names of the original stations between the terminals, going north, were Clark's Summit, Abington, Factoryville, Tunnel, Tunkhannock, Hop Bottom, Oakleys, Montrose, and New Milford.

The rails weighed 56 pounds to the yard and were laid on hemlock ties. There were no fishplates, but there was a cast-iron chair at each joint with an extra heavy tie beneath it.

During the construction of the road, there occurred a welcome interlude for the Irish. There were two gangs of these irrepressible people working in the vicinity of Clark's Summit. One was composed wholly of Northern Protestants and the other, also wholly, of Southern Catholics. Each group took a solemn oath to drive the other off the job. A pitched battle was fought after work on the evening of May 28, more than 150 men taking joyous part. There was one fatality on the field, two bodies were found in the bushes later on, a score of skulls were cracked, and numerous arms and legs broken. The "war" was at its merriest when George Scranton, hurriedly called to the scene, successfully pleaded with the antagonists to "break it up." After that, the two groups became sound friends and drinking companions, regaling other people nightly with ever-growing tall tales of "the diversion."

The first through train from Great Bend to Scranton, on October 15, 1851, was drawn by the engine "Wyoming." This engine was well-proportioned and weighed about 29 tons. It had the Stephenson link motion and the original stack was of the French and Baird design, but this was later removed and a Radley and Hunter stack substituted. Radley and Hunter purchased the patent rights of the French and Baird design and introduced some improvements of their own, which they had patented in January, 1850. The V-shaped circles, a prominent feature of the French and Baird stack, were discarded, thus improving the draft. This Radley and Hunter stack was in general use over the ensuing three-quarters of a century.

The engineer of the "Wyoming" was Francis A. Brown, and his train consisted of half a dozen coaches and flatcars which waited at Great Bend for the coming of the New York managers; these gentlemen arrived on the regular Erie Railroad train. The Lackawanna and Western train then started for Scranton, coaches and flatcars loaded with managers and well-wishers. A good run of about three hours was made, including two stops for wood and water. The day was warm and pleasant, and a great crowd of people awaited the special's arrival, a platform having been erected at the south end of the Lackawanna bridge for the accommodation of invited guests. President Phelps and George Scranton made speeches, and William Dodge offered a prayer of thanks to the Almighty. Engineer Brown, who left a few notes for posterity, related that on the return journey to Great Bend the "Wyoming" ran out of steam and "laid down." The cause of the stop was the "patent" smokestack, the perforated deflecting plates of which had become clogged with ashes, obstructing the draft. Mr. Brown opened the smokebox door to allow the smoke to escape and told his fireman to climb up to the stack with a hammer and cold chisel and knock some holes in the V-shaped circles.

When the sound of hammering was heard after the halt, George Scranton jumped from one of the cars and hurried up to the engine. Brown explained why the fireman was knocking holes in the stack and suggested that in the future the perforations be made larger. Mr. Scranton agreed—and switched to Radley and Hunter stacks. The journey was resumed with the now-ventilated stack functioning, and the party arrived at Great Bend just in time for the Erie train for New York—to the great satisfaction of the managers, who had feared they would miss it and thus be delayed in the wilds a whole day.

The road was opened for regular traffic on Monday, October 20, 1851, and Superintendent Dotterer made out a timetable for the one passenger train, which was in charge of Conductor Marcus Blair (a son of John I. Blair) and Engineer Brown. The three freight engines, soon to be doubled in number, were already busy moving previously ordered coal north and northwest. The passenger train left Scranton at nine in the morning, arriving at Great Bend at half past eleven. Returning, it was scheduled to leave Great Bend at six in the evening, provided the Erie train from New York was on time. However, the Erie was frequently late, and usually passengers did not get to Scranton until midnight. The solitary water tank was at a stream near a point called La Plume, and when this froze up, the train would either be stalled or drift into Scranton with the water level nearly on the crown sheet of the firebox.

9   *The Morris and Essex*

DURING the afternoon of April 7, 1849, the Senate and House of Representatives of the Commonwealth of Pennsylvania approved an act to incorporate the Delaware and Cobb's Gap Railroad Company, with a capital stock of 18,000 shares at $50 each. The following farmers, landowners, and businessmen—residents of the region to be traversed—were appointed commissioners to open books and receive subscriptions: Moses W. Coolbaugh, Simeon W. Schoonover, Thomas Grattan, Henry M. Labor, Adam Overfield, John Place, Benjamin Bush, Rudolphus Bingham, William Nyce, Samuel Taylor, and James H. Stroud.

As of December 4, 1849, Governor William F. Johnston of Pennsylvania issued a certificate to the Delaware and Cobb's Gap Railroad Company stating that "stipulations, conditions, and things in the aforesaid act directed to be performed have in all respects been fully complied with." This certificate carried a list of the subscribers to the stock. Among these were John I. Blair—1,000 shares; George W. Scranton—500 shares; Joseph H. Scranton—1,000 shares; Selden Scranton—467 shares; Joseph C. Platt—1,000 shares; Scrantons-Platt Company—1,000 shares; William E. Dodge—1,000 shares; John J. Phelps—1,000 shares; Anson G. Phelps—1,000 shares. Of the original applicants for incorporation only two appear as stock subscribers of record: James H. Stroud, of Stroudsburg, three shares; and Samuel Taylor, three shares.

As has been told in earlier chapters, Henry W. Drinker, former surveyor-general of Pennsylvania, turnpike builder, and speculator in potential coal-bearing lands, during the thirties had projected three plans for railroads to operate in the Lackawanna and Wyoming valleys, with coal carrying as their major objective. He had surveyed, or had had surveyed for him, three routes: first, the Lackawannack and Susquehanna line, to run from Scranton to Great Bend, which we have seen disposed of to George Scranton and his associates and becoming fact in the building of the Ligett's Gap Railroad; second, the Susquehanna and Delaware Canal and Railroad Company, to run from Delaware Water Gap to Wilkes-Barre, the line in which Drinker had interested Lord Charles Augustus Murray, and which was to carry coal from Drinker lands to the river and so to the eastern seaboard; and third, the Susquehanna Railroad, to run from Pittston to the New York state line. The last, in the Drinker form, never materialized.

Originally Drinker planned the second of his projected railroad lines to run up the Lackawanna River from Pittston to Roaring Brook, thence to Lake Henry, crossing the head springs of the Lehigh, and then down the Pocono and the Analomink to the Gap. Apparently he was dissatisfied with his first survey, for he engaged Major Ephraim Beech, a distinguished planner of railroads, to make another. Major Beech laid down a route which substantially followed the present right-of-way of the Delaware, Lackawanna and Western Railroad from Scranton to the Delaware River. The Beech survey was filed, along with the charter of the second Drinker railroad, and these documents lay in the files of the secretary of state until John Insley Blair stepped onto the stage.

When the Ligett's Gap Railroad, midway through construction, changed its name to the Lackawanna and Western Railroad, John Blair, already a director, was appointed its land agent. His duties were to secure right-of-way by means of outright purchase, by stock distribution in return for land, and by appeals to the courts and to arbitration boards when landowners were reluctant to part with their property or held out for prices which in his judgment were considered "iniquitous." *

* Official sympathy in those days seemed always to have been on the side of the railroads, but John Blair, smoothest of persuaders, appears invariably to have arranged matters amiably with the owners. Later he was to achieve the peak of his fame in securing gigantic land grants for the western roads which he was to build himself or in which he was to be associated with others.

The coal-carrying railroad plans of George Scranton, John Blair, Anson Phelps, and William E. Dodge were not to stop short with the Ligett's Gap road, the connection with the Erie to the northwest and the purchase and refurbishing of the Cayuga and Susquehanna. Of even more importance, in those times, was a route to tidewater and the seaboard market. John Blair—his chain stores, flour mills, and cotton factories efficiently operated by his numerous brothers and cousins—turned his time and his splendid brain and energy wholly to the development of the Lackawanna and Western.

On March 19, 1849, George Scranton and his associates took over the charter of the Ligett's Gap Railroad, as already told. Exactly three weeks later, on April 7, a group of local farmers and businessmen was granted incorporation of the Delaware and Cobb's Gap Railroad. The record of this incorporation was not published by the state until the summer of 1851. When the office of the secretary of state was later called on for an explanation, the answer was given that for two years the tax had not been paid and that therefore the matter had no standing. But the purchase of right-of-way went merrily along.

This secreted charter granted the right to build a railroad beginning at the Delaware River, "at or near the Delaware Water Gap," to a point terminating at or near Cobb's Gap (six miles southeast of Scranton); the charter extended the southern terminus of the road down the Delaware River so as to connect with the Belvidere and Delaware Railroad and, for this purpose, granted permission to construct a bridge across the river.

On November 28, 1850, while the act of incorporation was still presumably awaiting implementation and publication because of nonpayment of the tax, a meeting of the commissioners of the Delaware and Cobb's Gap Railroad was held in Stroudsburg at the home of Jacob Knecht, a prominent citizen but not, in so far as the records show, one of the commissioners. Also present were George Scranton, John Blair, William E. Dodge and George D. Phelps, president of the Lackawanna and Western, none of whom were commissioners.

If any minutes of this extraordinary meeting were kept, they have long since disappeared. But three important matters were acted on: (1) a decision to apply for a charter was approved; (2) the 18,000 shares, priced at $50 apiece, were subscribed; (3) George Scranton was elected president of the Delaware and Cobb's Gap Railroad. Eight days later, on December 4, Governor Johnston granted the charter.

With the publication of this document, Henry Drinker woke up! This was *his* railroad! True, the name had been changed, but this was the route he had paid Ephraim Beech to survey. A very old man, he had been letting things slip, had been taking little interest in matters outside his own garden gate. Drinker grabbed his sticks and hobbled out into the world, to find that John Blair had made secure the right-of-way, that teams of workmen were already hacking at the trees, that Chief Engineer Edwin McNeil was piling T rail.

Poor old Henry didn't have much of a case—in the legal sense. He had allowed his charter to lapse. But he had a certain nuisance value; in court he would eventually lose, but he could go into court and, quite possibly, delay matters. Mr. Blair was well aware that the Morris and Essex Railroad, coming up from Hoboken, had already applied to the New Jersey Legislature to build from Dover "to any point on the Delaware River at or near the town of Belvidere or the Water Gap." Mr. Blair knew—if Henry Drinker did not—that the Morris and Essex would get this supplement to its charter; and, in plain language, he was after the Morris and Essex. As Blair saw things, that road would eventually either engulf the Lackawanna and Western, or vice versa. Blair went to visit old Henry, read him a lecture on his duties as a stockholder to the Lackawanna and Western, laid $1,000 on the table, and left with a signed quitclaim.

Beyond hacking at the forest, little work was done on the Cobb's Gap line over the next two years. John Blair, after some deep thinking, had decided to play cat-and-mouse with the Morris and Essex Railroad.

On January 29, 1835, a group of New York, Newark, and Philadelphia businessmen—James Cook, William N. Wood, William Brittin, Jephtha P. Munn, Israel D. Condit, John I. Bryans, and Isaac Baldwin, the railroad-engine builder—were given a charter by the Council and General Assembly of New Jersey for the purpose of forming a corporation to construct a railroad from Morristown, New Jersey, to "some point in Essex County contiguous to the tide-

The Morris and Essex Railroad (Incorporated January 29, 1835),
acquisition of which brought the Lackawanna to the seaboard

water, near the harbor of New York, in such a manner as to facilitate
the intercourse between the country and the city."

Capital stock was authorized at $300,000, with permission to in-
crease to $500,000. Jersey folk were anxious for a closer link with
the big harbor and the growing city, and the money was quickly
forthcoming. Benjamin Wright was chosen as the builder, and Ma-

jor Ephraim Beech, engineer and surveyor, became his associate. These two experts made a report that "a good road for either horse or steam power" could be constructed for $9,000 a mile, this to include a $20,000 bridge over the Passaic river. The road would be strap and the gauge 4 feet, 10 inches.

This report was based on building the road from Morristown to a point intersecting the line of the New Jersey Railroad and Transportation Company (now the Pennsylvania Railroad) at Newark or Elizabethtown (now Elizabeth). Following the submission of the report, Major Beech, along with one of the original incorporators, William Brittin, took over the construction contract; the cost was set at $114,597.88 and the contractors agreed to take one-third of their pay in stock.

An interesting provision of the contract as signed between the builders and the railroad, represented by President Lewis Condit, as ardent a prohibitionist as William E. Dodge, follows:

For the preservation of peace and good order, to prevent riots and brawls and other disturbances along the line of this work, it is mutually agreed that no ardent spirits nor any kind of intoxicating drink shall be permitted by the contractors, who hereby pledge themselves to use all proper endeavors and to exert their best influence to prevent its introduction and use among the laborers employed on the work.

Construction went along apace, but whether speed was due to the ruling regarding temperance is not recorded. On November 19, 1836, a sharp, early-winter day, the road was officially opened from Morristown to Orange; there was one car, drawn by horses. The driver-conductor was Andrew O. Crane, a Hoboken-born man. Two daily trips each way were made, and the fare was fifteen cents with no reduction for a round trip. You paid as you rode, and Mr. Crane kept collections for two weeks before turning them in. There is no explanation as to why he was allowed to do this, but possibly he persuaded the management that he had to have plenty of change on hand.

Nobody seemed to worry about footpads or holdup men, and every second Saturday Mr. Crane handed over something between $50 and $80. His salary was $30 a month. An excellent Jehu, he drove his horses without accident, as the line extended itself over the next eight months, and when the first locomotive of the Morris and Essex, called "Orange," showed up in the late summer of 1837, Mr. Crane was appointed wood passer.

"Orange" was built by Seth Boyden, of Newark, an ingenious fellow credited with the invention of an early governor which controlled engine steam by a slide valve, instead of by a throttle. The principal dimensions of "Orange" were: cylinders, 8¼ inches in diameter, by 26-inch stroke; driving wheels, 53½ inches in diameter; truck wheels, 3½ inches in diameter; the wheel hubs, 18 inches and 10 inches in diameter respectively. The last were highly polished, solid cast iron with central strengthening ribs painted bright blue; the rest of the wheel was bright red.

The valve motion (Mr. Boyden's invention) was worked full stroke and was reversed by moving the eccentric rod, with a return crank, to either end of a V box fastened to the rocker shaft. The lever pivoted to the upright post which carried a flat spring with an eye, through which passed the eccentric rod. This description is taken from notes made by Seth Boyden's son, Obadiah. Mr. Boyden used no drawings in building "Orange."

The engine was first tried out on a beautiful summer afternoon, July 31, 1837, and folk from all around gathered in Newark to see the exhibition. Builder Boyden had got "Orange" to the Morris and Essex tracks on Broad Street by building a temporary track from his shop. He was assisted at the engine by David Harris, chief engineer of the Newark Sewerage Pumping Works. Young Obadiah Boyden was wood passer; Andy Crane had not yet been promoted —or, perhaps, in his own opinion, demoted—to the latter job and was still driving his horses.

The arrival of brightly colored "Orange" on the railroad tracks was greeted with the combined music of four bands and the cheers of all Newark and points adjacent. This was the town's own railroad, and its people had stood solidly behind its construction with a subscription of one-third of the capital stock and the gift of free passage over Broad Street to the Passaic River bridge.

The directors of the Morris and Essex, silk-hatted and Prince-Albert-coated, awaited the arrival of the 6-ton engine and its two empty cars on the top of Newark Hill; as enthusiastic as their fellow citizens, they were at the same time more cautious. Adventurous citizens sought to clamber aboard the train at its start, but the cars were kept empty for the directors, who apparently wanted to see first what would happen.

The engine ran beautifully but noisily, drowning out the cheers of the populace and the triumphal music of the massed bands, and breasted the hill. Unable to hear the congratulations of the directors above the noise of escaping steam, Mr. Boyden placed his hand on his safety-valve lever.

The boiler shook and trembled! Then the whole engine shimmied! The directors, as one man, galloped downhill as fast as their legs would carry them! Boyden, his son, and Sewerage-expert Harris remained at their posts. Steam was shut off, and "Orange" rolled smoothly back into Newark; the copper dry pipe, too thin, had collapsed. Mr. Boyden replaced it with a heavier one and all was well. On October 2, 1837, regular steam service was inaugurated between Madison and Newark, and Mr. Crane became wood passer.

Of interest to the vast army of commuting patrons of the Delaware, Lackawanna and Western, who now ride from their New York offices to their suburban homes and back again over what was the Morris and Essex, is the water-taking facility for "Orange" and its immediate successors, "Essex" and "Cometa," also built by Seth Boyden. "Orange" first took water at Millville (now Milburn), drawing it from a millpond alongside the track; but it was soon learned that the engine, with a full water load, could not carry the extra weight up the 80-foot grade to Summit. Stephen Vail, of Morristown, a foundry owner, came to the rescue with a machine he built at Summit by which the engine itself could pump water from a well. Two large wheels were sunk below the track and in line with the rails, so that the driving wheels of the locomotive could rest on those of the sunken wheels; the engine was then lashed with chains, and the driving wheels revolved the large wheels, which were mounted on a shaft connected to the pumps.

In a story concerning "Orange" which appeared in the *American Railroad Journal* of August 26, 1837, the Morris and Essex is given credit for the first spark arrester, as well as a speed record. Flying sparks were one of the biggest bothers of early railroads.

The new and improved locomotive of the Morris and Essex railroad, constructed by Mr. Seth Boyden of Newark, goes at the rate of sixty to

seventy miles per hour [sic]. The passengers are wholly protected from
the fire of the chimney; the sparks are taken . . . to the ashpan beneath.

According to memoranda left by Obadiah Boyden, his father
had placed a wire netting in the smokebox of "Orange" just above
the top row of flues, and the ashes were removed through small slid-
ing doors in the smokebox front. Crude, as Obadiah Boyden ad-
mits, it was still the first spark arrester on record and the description
of the device must be given more credence than the "sixty to seventy
miles per hour." Ten miles would be more like it.

Newark, in the eighteen thirties, was a quiet, leisurely place, despite the fact that merchants were awaking to the importance of
their town as a near neighbor to the already-great metropolis over
the Hudson River and its own strategic value as a business and industrial feeder to growing Essex County and the lands beyond.
In the fashion of their time these middle-nineteenth-century New-
arkians considered themselves hustlers.

The town's greatest pride was its own railroad, the Morris and
Essex; and the two big events of the day were the arrival and de-
parture of the train that ran between Newark and Morristown.
"Orange" hauled two small cars, wooden-wheeled, with iron tires
and hubs. Baggage was carried in a "boot" under the cars.

Leaving Newark, rarely with more than a dozen passengers, the
early crew consisted of Henry L. Brown, engine driver; William
Osborn, fireman; Andrew O. Crane, wood passer; Benjamin Myers,
conductor. If Mr. Crane had any regrets over losing his horses, he
must have been relieved to learn that he was to retain them; when
the train passed through Newark, he took over the "throttle," in
the form of reins, and on this short ride he functioned again as conductor. Some folk were wont to climb aboard on the "horse division," and Mr. Crane had his leather bag and small change ready.

The preparations for leaving Newark were impressive. Fireman
Osborn and Wood-passer Crane, each provided with a spouted
bucket of sand, seated themselves on the front beam of "Orange,"
and the train would then back down from the curve at Broad Street
as far as Orange Street, sand pouring on the tracks from the spouts
"to give a grip." Yelling small boys and squealing little girls followed the backward course of the train delightedly, while their

elders, just as deeply interested, sat on doorsteps enjoying the show.

The great journey commenced, with fresh sand still pouring from the bucket spouts. If there was only one car to haul, "Orange" would go it alone. If there were two cars, the first one would be hauled up Newark Hill and left at the Nesbitt Street switch, while "Orange" slid back for the other, the sanding operation being continued. Later on, when "Essex" arrived to help "Orange," one engine would pull, while the other would push, and between them they usually managed to make it in fine style. There were no arguments or complaints from the passengers regarding service. This was an event in their lives and they were out to enjoy it to the full. There were five stops—Orange, Millville, Summit, Chatham, and Madison—and now and again, particularly if the minister wanted a ride, there was a halt at the Brick Church. Later, Mountain Road was made a stop; this is now the South Orange station.

On the return journey the train sometimes ran away down Newark Hill and over Broad and Market Streets. The brake, in the tender of "Orange," was primitive—an upright rod with a step on its lower end. The fireman would unhook the rod, stand on the step, and press down. Sometimes it did not work so well, and "Orange" went wild, terrorizing pedestrians and smashing wagons and carriages. After a while Newark came to realize that the tracks were not a safe place to be when the Morris and Essex rolled in from Morristown. Always, whether running away or not, the engineer steamburst a warning to clear the track.

Arriving in Newark, Wood-passer Crane would leap from the tender, hitch horses to the car, and drive down Broad Street and Market Street to the depot of the New Jersey Railroad and Transportation Company. There passengers and baggage would be transferred to the train for New York.

Conductor-Engineer-Wood-passer Crane's "conductor book" has been preserved for posterity. Entries are illustrative of business, or the lack of it!

Monday, Feb. 26, 1838—12 passengers carried.
Tuesday—three passengers.
Wednesday—one passenger.
Thursday—car ran empty.
Friday—five passengers.
Saturday—six passengers.

Two trains were run each way daily, but there were no Sunday trains. Little boys, and sometimes their elders, made a practice of jumping on and off the cars as they moved along, and in so far as the record shows, never succeeded in hurting themselves. The engines had no whistles, the only signal of approach and warning being the raising of the safety-valve spring balance, permitting steam to blow off. The trains always halted for cows or grazing horses, the reason being not so much concern for the cow or horse as the certainty that the train would be derailed and that, if cow or horse were so much as scratched, the owner would sue for damages. Another of Andy Crane's multitudinous jobs was to shoo geese off the track.

The first freight train of the Morris and Essex pulled out of Newark for Morristown on the afternoon of July 20, 1838. "Orange" pulled a single heavily loaded car, and "Essex" pushed. The load was soap and flour, and the occasion marked Andy Crane's induction at long last into a steady routine; he was appointed the road's first combination freight-conductor-and-brakeman.

10   *Coal to Seaboard*

On March 11, 1853, the Pennsylvania Legislature approved a joint application made by the Lackawanna and Western Railroad Company (the Ligett's Gap Railroad) and the Delaware and Cobb's Gap Railroad Company for a consolidation under the corporate name of the Delaware, Lackawanna and Western Railroad Company. George D. Phelps was elected president of the new organization, and books were opened for subscriptions to increase the capital stock; this at the time amounted to $1,441,000, and $1,-500,000 additional was sold within a week. The survey had already been made, payments were completed on right-of-way purchases, and the Cobb's Gap road became the southern division of the Lackawanna.

At the time of the first merger there was not a town of any size —Stroudsburg was a mere village—between the Delaware Water Gap and the thriving coal and iron mart of Scranton. Chief Engineer Edwin McNeil, veteran of the Ligett's Gap job, had a tough assignment ahead of him. The forests of the Blue Mountains were deep and thickly wooded, and the line had to be driven right through the heart of this tremendous obstacle. And there was Mount Pocono to be negotiated, a formidable undertaking from an engineering point of view. The region to be traversed was still remote from lines of communication, as they existed in those days, and from the supply markets. Labor was difficult to get because of this inaccessibility, and grading and masonry contracts came high. But the Lackawanna paid the prices demanded, and work went ahead on the southern division, as well as on the Tunkhannock Tunnel, still a-building on the northern division (Ligett's Gap).

Cost of construction and equipment during the year 1853 far exceeded the original estimates. Disbursements were $2,162,048.75. Items which had to be taken care of were right-of-way purchase completions, T rail, buildings and office expenses, tracklaying, the tunnel job, 13 locomotives, 10 passenger and baggage cars, 60 house and platform freight cars, 854 coal cars, erection of machine and car shops and their equipment.

Before the southern division (1856) and the Tunkhannock Tunnel (1854) could be completed, a first mortgage of $1,500,000 was placed on the line, and then a second mortgage of $2,600,000. At this time the Scrantons-Platt Company became the Lackawanna Iron and Coal Company and was operated coordinately with the Lackawanna, though under separate ownership. The cash refreshers were engineered by Moses Taylor, of the Lackawanna Board and head of the National City Bank of New York. This bank was a heavy investor in coal lands in the region. Mr. Taylor was out to sell the public on anthracite, against which, at the time, there was still much prejudice as "hard to burn." The Lackawanna was still using wood-burning engines, though coal burners were fast coming into use. Here was still another argument in the mind of the public against general use of anthracite: Why, if it was such a good thing, didn't the Lackawanna use it instead of the green, unseasoned wood which made liars of time schedules? The road itself owned 2,500 acres of coal lands, which, so far, had been worked on contract. On October 19, 1853, the Lackawanna ordered its first coal-burning engine.

In April, 1852, Moses Taylor arranged the financing and incorporation of the Lackawanna and Bloomsburg Railroad Company, to run from Scranton to Bloomsburg, tapping the rich Luzerne County (Wyoming Valley) coal basin, and to connect with the Lackawanna at Scranton. The Lackawanna and Bloomsburg was merged with the Lackawanna, June 16, 1873.

Moses Taylor—ably assisted, of course, by John Blair, William E. Dodge, and George Scranton—lifted the Lackawanna into a strategic position in the anthracite-coal trade; he originated a "coal department," which bought heavily of advertising space in the newspapers and even gave away carloads of coal to reluctant industrialists. This advertising and give-away program reached its height in the spring of 1856, for on May 27 of that year the southern division of the Lackawanna was formally opened from Scranton to the Delaware River, crossing the water over its new bridge at Delaware.

During the construction of the southern division, the Board of Managers of the Lackawanna had negotiated a contract with the Central Railroad of New Jersey to haul coal and other freight at one and one-fourth cents per ton-mile from New Hampton (Hampton), New Jersey, to Elizabethport on New York Harbor. Thus the Lackawanna was to reach the eastern seaboard. A third rail was built to accommodate the Lackawanna broad-gauge cars. A gap of some 18 miles between the two lines was covered by the Warren Railroad Company, the brain child of that irrepressible manipulator of railroad promotions, mergers, and consolidations, John Blair.

Following the agreement between the Central of New Jersey and the Lackawanna (1854), Blair started to build the Warren in the spring of 1855. It was open for traffic June 10, 1856, just two weeks after the completion of the Lackawanna's southern division. Purchases—and gifts—of coal started rolling immediately over this necessary avenue to the eastern seaboard market. On October 1, following, the Warren Railroad was leased in perpetuity to the Lackawanna.

Mr. Blair had finally outwitted the Morris and Essex—and the story is worth going back a few years to relate.

By the summer of 1848 the Morris and Essex, then a T railroad, had extended its line from Morristown as far as Dover and planned eventually to build to Phillipsburg through Hackettstown. The Warren Railroad crossed the tracks of the Morris and Essex midway between Bridgeville and Broadway. Here was where the Morris and Essex planned to build west toward the Lackawanna Valley coal fields; but its directors did not put their thoughts into action fast enough, and when they did go to work, they found themselves up against a faster worker, in the person of John Blair.

As of February 19, 1851, the New Jersey Legislature granted the Morris and Essex an extension of its railroad "from some point at or near Dover in the county of Morris to any point on the Delaware River at or near the town of Belvidere or the Water Gap and with power to construct a bridge or bridges across the river by and with the consent of the State of Pennsylvania."

As of February 12, 1851, just one week before the Morris and Essex grant, the same legislature granted an act of incorporation to the Warren Railroad Company "to survey, lay out and construct a railroad from some suitable place on the Delaware River, not more than five miles from the Delaware Water Gap, by the most feasible route, to intersect the Central Railroad Company of New Jersey, at or near New Hampton, situate in the county of Hunterdon with a branch to Belvidere in the county of Warren."

The charters outlined practically parallel routes; the building of one would defeat the purpose of the other, so that there was no sense in building both roads. The powers behind the Warren charter were camouflaged in the persons of a group of little-known business-men. Although the Warren's permission to build had been granted a week earlier than that of the Morris and Essex, the latter was an established road, merely asking for an extension, while the Warren had to open subscription books, dispose of its stock, and elect officers, before it could function. The day after its extension grant had been approved, officials of the Morris and Essex arrived at the office of the secretary of state at Trenton to sign the necessary papers. There, to their indignation and chagrin, they found John Blair, newly elected president and newly appointed land agent of the Warren Railroad, with proofs of $400,000 worth of stock sold and delivered.

The next day Blair and his antagonists were on the Delaware se-curing rights-of-way, a much easier job for Blair than for the Morris and Essex officials, for here he was on his own home grounds; and, although there is no record to that effect, he undoubtedly had picked his spots long since, with the blessing of the Lackawanna. Blair had everything he needed below the Water Gap. The Morris and Essex people, although they must have known of Blair's connections with the Lackawanna, struck for passage in and above the Gap on the New Jersey side, paying exorbitant sums to farmers and for two contemplated bridge sites.

The southern division of the Lackawanna, still building at the time, came down through the Gap on the Pennsylvania side and crossed the river several miles below, leaving the Morris and Essex with its high-priced passes and crosses on its hands. On October 1,

1857, the Lackawanna leased the Warren Railroad in perpetuity, on a guarantee of payment of 7 per cent annually on the stock investment.

The directors signing for the Warren Railroad were our old friends, John Blair, William E. Dodge, and George Scranton. As all three were also directors of the Lackawanna, they could have signed for that road, too. But apparently it was considered better to have other signatures. C. R. Robert, who had succeeded George Phelps as president of the Lackawanna, affixed his signature, as did the road's secretary, A. J. Odell. Mr. Blair would have begun construction on the Warren earlier than he did (1855) but for the fact that the Morris and Essex attorneys tied him up in court and in appeals to the legislature. Blair won. With the matter finally settled and the link between the Lackawanna and the Central of New Jersey complete, John Blair went west to lay an all-rail route between Chicago and Cedar Rapids and grab his first land grant from the Mississippi River to Council Bluffs.* But Gravel Hill, now Blairstown, was his home, and although he strayed far, he returned at regular intervals.

The Morris and Essex, at the time it attempted to outwit John Blair, had been having an era of prosperity. At first it had failed to gather up enough business to bring in even costs of operation, and the Newark businessmen who had put it on the map forsook it. The road was reorganized by New York financiers, steam operation replaced the horses on the Newark streets, and a contract was made with the New Jersey Railroad and Transportation Company whereby, for $25,000 a year, the latter hauled the Morris and Essex cars into Jersey City. By the time the line reached Hackettstown (1854), its financial condition was sound, its traffic revenue being mostly derived from minerals—iron, zinc, and limestone. Nobody then paid much attention to the romantic scenery of the Kittatinny Mountains, so attractive to Lackawanna tourists and pleasure seekers today, and the region was not yet a commuter's paradise.

In 1860, the Morris and Essex, by then paying dividends, completed its extension from Hackettstown to Easton on the Delaware and built a branch from Dover to the Water Gap, by means of which it was at long last able to corral some coal traffic from the Lacka-

* Casey and Douglas, *Pioneer Railroad*, McGraw-Hill Book Company, Inc., New York.

wanna. With the end of the Civil War and the resumption of normal business, the line was in a good strategic position as regarded railroad consolidation. It had a through road from the Delaware River to Newark and attracted the attention of Samuel L'Hommedieu, president of the Atlantic and Great Western Railroad, who was seeking to tap the oil fields of northwestern Pennsylvania and Ohio as the Lackawanna was tapping the coal fields of the northeast. L'Hommedieu executed a lease with the Morris and Essex as part of an ambitious new trunk line from Dayton, Ohio, to the eastern seaboard; but the Atlantic and Great Western had a flimsy financial structure and collapsed before it was able to take over the Morris and Essex.

The latter, saved from disaster by the slow deliberation of its directors, found itself able, however, to reach Hoboken—and New York Harbor—because of the ambitions of another railroad manipulator. This was Edwin A. Stevens, owner of the wealthy Camden and Amboy road, which had a monopoly of the New York–Philadelphia business. A battle was developing between Stevens and the New Jersey Railroad Company, a prosperous short line between New Brunswick and Jersey City.*

The New Jersey Railroad was out to break Stevens' monopoly by extending itself to the Delaware River between Trenton and Easton. Stevens held a franchise, which he had never exercised, to lay track from Newark to Hoboken, paralleling the New Jersey road. He bought heavily into the Morris and Essex and then sold it the Newark-Hoboken franchise on which the Morris and Essex built into Hoboken. By this move Stevens hoped to undermine the New Jersey Railroad and eliminate competition to Philadelphia. The Morris and Essex got its line through from Easton to Hoboken but overstepped itself financially.

Fixed charges jumped from $37,506 in 1864 to $350,000 in 1867. The postwar slump was on and earnings failed to keep abreast of the growing indebtedness. In four years the bonded debt had grown from $340,000 to $6,347,437. The Lackawanna, with plenty of money in its treasury, was making up its mind about its own passage to the sea. The road had three choices: It could buy the Morris

* Bogen, John I., *History of the Anthracite Railroads*, The Macmillan Company, New York.

Canal, but canals were becoming back numbers in the interests of speed. It could purchase its present hauler from the Delaware to the seaboard, the Central of New Jersey, but this road was making money and the price would be high. Or it could make a deal with the debt-burdened Morris and Essex.

On February 9, 1869, an agreement was executed, whereby the Lackawanna took over the Morris and Essex on a perpetual rental basis equal to a 7 per cent dividend rate on the capitalization. Included was a proviso that rebuilding, extension, and improvements made under the Morris and Essex franchise were to be covered through the issue of bonds and stocks guaranteed *pari passu* with the outstanding shares.* The agreement covered the Newark and Bloomfield and the Chester Railroads—Morris and Essex properties.

The Lackawanna started immediately on a rejuvenating job. The Morris and Essex capitalization at the time of the lease was $13,891,-555 in stocks and bonds. Additional stocks and bonds were sold almost at once to bring the total to $19,659,100; in 1871 this was increased to $24,084,950. A new main line was put in, specially designed for freight and coal traffic, from Denville, New Jersey, through Paterson and Passaic to rejoin the old route at Hoboken. A tunnel was cut through the Bergen Hills, and a third track was laid to accommodate the Lackawanna broad-gauge cars.

But while the Lackawanna was doing its face-lifting job on the Morris and Essex, the Central Railroad of New Jersey refused to take the deal other than seriously. Since 1854, as will be recalled, there had been a traffic contract between the Lackawanna and the Central, whereby the latter had been hauling to the seaboard the coal delivered to it over the Lackawanna's leased road, the Warren. The arrangement had been made when George D. Phelps was president of the Lackawanna, and the perpetual rental of the Morris and Essex had been put through by Samuel Sloan, who, elected to the presidency in August, 1867, guided the ever-increasing fortunes of his road for just five months short of thirty-two years.

Following the tremendous profits accruing to the anthracite coal industry during and immediately after the Civil War, all competing railroads, as well as railroads with connection arrangements to and

---

* Bogen, John I., *History of the Anthracite Railroads*, The Macmillan Company, New York.

from the coal fields, plunged into the market to buy or lease coal-bearing or potentially coal-bearing lands. The Delaware and Hudson increased its already large holdings to the north, and the Central of New Jersey was buying wherever it could; it was bidding up on land which, if coal came out of it, would be served by the Lackawanna.

The charters of the big coal-hauling and coal-owning roads, such as the Delaware and Hudson, the Philadelphia and Reading, the Lackawanna, the Lehigh Valley, and the Pennsylvania, carried clauses limiting ownership of coal lands by any one railroad to 1,000 acres; in the fifties this was increased to 2,000 acres. But soon after this extra acreage had been approved, the state announced a policy of refusing charters to any contemplated road which also sought coal-mine ownership privileges. This stand was in all probability due to objection—call it lobbying, if you will—by those powerful carriers already in possession of their coal fields.

The embargo on new coal roads did not prevent those existing lines from acquiring coal companies by buying up their capital stock, and those who could afford to do so went into action. Moses Taylor, John J. Phelps, William E. Dodge, John I. Blair, George and Selden Scranton, John Brisbin, and Percy Pyne (Taylor's son-in-law), all directors and heavy stockholders in the Lackawanna, had either secured control of existing coal companies or had bought land and formed companies. Between 1865 and 1868 the Lackawanna purchased the Continental Coal Company—along with its little carrier, the Keyser Valley Railroad Company—the Scranton Coal Company, the Steuben Coal Company, and the Granby Coal Company and had merged them all with the Nanticoke Coal Company.

On June 23, 1870, an agreement was signed to consolidate and merge the Nanticoke Coal Company with the Delaware, Lackawanna and Western Railroad, the holders of Nanticoke stock receiving dollar for dollar of Lackawanna stock in exchange for their certificates. Those signing for the Lackawanna were: Sam Sloan, president; Charles E. Carryl, secretary; S. B. Chittenden; Moses Taylor; George Bulkley; Percy R. Pyne; William E. Dodge; Denning Duer; George Bliss; John Brisbin; John I. Blair; Wilson G. Hunt; William Walter Phelps; and R. R. Graves.

The signers for the Nanticoke Coal Company were: John C.

Phelps, president; Charles E. Carryl, secretary; Moses Taylor; William E. Dodge; John I. Blair; James Archbald; John Brisbin; and William Walter Phelps. "An envious, carping tongue"—to quote the Bard—might call this too much of a family affair, but if it was a good thing for the signers, it was also a good thing for even the smallest stockholder in the railroad. The Lackawanna gathered in more than 25,000 acres of the richest coal-bearing lands in the anthracite belt, and every single black nut was on or adjacent to its trackage.

This coal deal, on top of the Lackawanna's taking over of the Morris and Essex, decided the directors of the Central of New Jersey in the matter of action. They brought suit to enforce the 1854 traffic contract, under which the Central had laid down a third rail to accommodate the broader gauge of the Lackawanna cars. President Sloan did all he could to soothe and smother the indignation of the Central directorate. Both roads were making money. The country was growing and the demand for coal was increasing with it. Within the carrying zones of both lines villages and hamlets were growing almost overnight into towns and cities. Factories, industrial plants, and workshops had increased more than a hundredfold since the North and the South had laid down arms.

Mr. Sloan suggested a consolidation. The combined assets of the Lackawanna and the Central were valued at $120,000,000. The Central directors, headed by President John Taylor Johnston, were impressed with the Sloan arguments. On March 16, 1872, an agreement was signed, whereby "the entire railroads, properties, and interests now held by said companies . . . and hereafter . . . built or acquired shall be forever operated and managed as a joint estate, and under the joint management hereafter provided for." *

Each company was to retain its individual organization, and a joint board was to be set up consisting of the two presidents and of five directors from each road. Net profits and losses were to be shared equally. Each company had $20,000,000 of common stock and the dividend rate was to be the same for both.†

It seemed to be a good plan; there was a community of interests

* Central Railroad of New Jersey, *Annual Report*, 1872.

† BOGEN, JOHN I., *History of the Anthracite Railroads*, The Macmillan Company, New York.

and a pool. But dissension soon broke out among the opposing directors. The Lackawanna refused to alter its broad gauge, contending that the Central should lay a third track all over its system; it also insisted on selling coal at public auction at the pit head and at seaboard, instead of setting prices as the Central wished to do with its own coal. Another matter which particularly incensed the Central was the issuance by the Lackawanna, immediately after the merger had been signed, of $3,000,000 of convertible 7 per cent bonds. The Central declared the agreement voided on the technical ground that it had not been properly recorded. The Lackawanna went into court, seeking to enforce the merger, but lost its case—which, in so far as it was concerned, was all to the good, for two years later the Central of New Jersey dropped into the hands of the receivers.

11 *Steel Rails and*
Narrow Gauge

IF the formative years of the Lackawanna and its emergence as a great coal carrier are to be credited—as they should be—to George Scranton and John I. Blair, then the development years, the acquisition of the lines of communication which brought it the status of a trunk line and a general carrier, belong to Samuel Sloan, Irish immigrant and former tracklayer, who guided the destinies of his beloved railroad for more than three decades.

On March 3, 1869, a group of men gathered in the office of Moses Taylor at the National City Bank in New York, of which Mr. Taylor was president. Among those present were his following co-managers (directors) of the Lackawanna: Samuel Sloan, John J. Phelps, John Brisbin, Percy R. Pyne, George Bulkley, William Walter Phelps, Charles E. Carryl (secretary of the Lackawanna), and George Bliss.

The purpose was the forging of a very necessary link in the Lackawanna's railroad chain. We have seen that the northern division (the old Ligett's Gap road) reached Great Bend, at which point Lackawanna loads destined for the Great Lakes region and beyond were transferred to the tracks of the Erie.

Three weeks before the meeting at the National City Bank the Lackawanna had purchased the capital stock of the Syracuse, Binghamton and New York Railroad Company. Back in 1858 it had acquired from George Scranton and William E. Dodge the Cayuga and Susquehanna Railroad, originally the Ithaca and Owego, which furnished access to the Erie Canal by means of the rental agreement with the Erie Railroad.

Thus, when Mr. Taylor met with his co-managers, the Lackawanna had two entries to the north, but their loads still had to get there over the Erie tracks. They were met to solve the problem of the 11-mile gap between the Great Bend terminus of the Lackawanna's northern division and the newly acquired Syracuse, Bing-

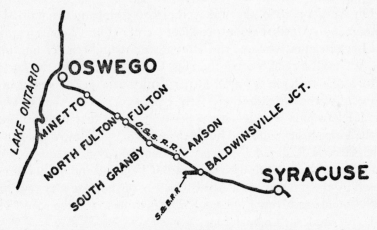

The Oswego and Syracuse Railroad (Incorporated 1839), first Great Lakes contact of the Lackawanna

hamton and New York line. On March 1, two days before the gathering of the clans in Mr. Taylor's office, the Lackawanna had also secured by lease the Oswego and Syracuse Railroad, connecting with the Syracuse, Binghamton and New York at Syracuse, thus securing connection from Binghamton to Lake Ontario. If that 11-mile gap were bridged, the Lackawanna might very well come to dispense with the services of the Erie Railroad.

The articles of association of the Valley Railroad Company, drawn up at the National City Bank meeting, provided that the proposed road "enable the association to make the most ready, convenient, and practical connections with the tracks and depots of the Erie Railway Company, the Syracuse, Binghamton and New

York Railroad Company, and the Albany and Susquehanna Railroad Company."

It was a shrewdly drawn document, worthy of John Blair at his best, carefully veiling the intention of Moses Taylor and Samuel Sloan, not only ultimately to do without the Erie, but to become its very worthy competitor. It furthered a plan of campaign which had been initiated by Blair and which was moving along splendidly, despite his absence in the West, where he was gathering together the short lines which eventually were to emerge as the far-flung Chicago and North Western Railroad system.*

On April 15, 1869, the Valley Railroad Company, capitalized at $1,000,000—Moses Taylor, president—entered into a contract with the Lackawanna, whereby the latter agreed to build the 11-mile line, the Valley Railroad footing the bills. On its completion, the Lackawanna was to lease the road in perpetuity at a yearly rental of 8 per cent of the capitalization—later 5 per cent. As of April 9, 1870, the Lackawanna leased—on a 6 per cent annual payment on stock —the Utica, Chenango and Susquehanna Valley Railway Company. The Greene Railroad Company, connecting the Syracuse, Binghamton and New York with the Utica, Chenango and Susquehanna, leased by the Lackawanna, April 26, 1870, opened the way to traffic with Canada and New England. Shippers came to call the road "The Atlantic and Lake Ontario Line."

With the beginning of the seventies the Lackawanna was emerging from a simple coal carrier to a general traffic line. It was now faced with two major construction problems: Steel rails were slowly but surely supplanting those of iron. The Lackawanna Iron and Coal Company had not as yet got round to the steel process; the road, like its competitors, had to look to England, as they all had looked to England for iron T rail at the beginning of the railroad era. The second problem was narrow gauge.

In the summer of 1871 the Lackawanna ordered its first shipment of steel rails from across the water—247 tons from the Perfect Dowlas Steel Company; in 1872, 2,846 tons were bought; in 1873, 2,286 tons; in 1874, 967 tons. By this time American production

* Casey and Douglas, *Pioneer Railroad*, McGraw-Hill Book Company, Inc., New York.

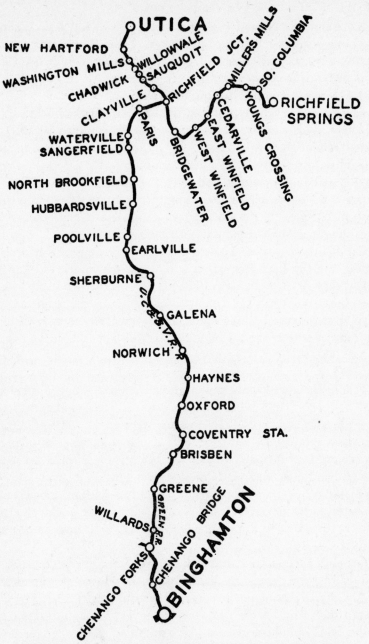

The Greene Railroad (Incorporated 1869) and the Utica, Chenango and Susquehanna Railroad (Incorporated 1866), which, linked to the Ligett's Gap Railroad at Binghamton, opened new coal markets for the Lackawanna

was moving along, and the Lackawanna held down its order. In 1875 the road purchased 4,240 tons of Troy American steel rails, and by 1876 the Lackawanna Iron and Coal Company had got itself into shape to make steel rail for its associate. All this rail, English and American, weighed 60 pounds to the yard.

Regarding the gauge problem, the Lackawanna had held steadily to 6 feet. As had been the case during its association with the Central of New Jersey, it had had to lay a third rail on some of its small bought or leased lines, which had been built to the 4-foot-8½-gauge rapidly becoming standard all over the continent. Mr. Sloan had foreseen the necessity for the change from broad to standard gauge with his election to the presidency, and since he had taken office, all rolling stock had been built with the switch in mind.

On March 15, 1876, a twenty-four-hour halt was called on all traffic, and the Lackawanna, over its right-of-way, bristled with a gigantic army of tracklayers. The change on the bed itself was accomplished in forty-eight hours, and traffic on the main line was delayed only twenty-four hours. It was one of the most amazing feats in American railroad-building history. The cost of the job was $1,250,000.

The Lackawanna, now a high-grade standard-gauge all-steel railroad operating from New York City to the Great Lakes, was running into stiff competition. Its position in the coal trade was enviable, not only as a carrier for hire, but as owner of some of the best deposits of anthracite. The job had been accomplished—when all was said and done—at a very modest expenditure; its leases of other roads had called only for payment of interest with little or no capital outlay. On the surface its bonded debt would cause no alarm; in 1875 this was $2,831,000, while capital stock outstanding was $25,889,000.

But under-the-surface figures were disquieting. The Lackawanna had guaranteed 7 per cent dividends on the Morris and Essex issue of $15,477,565 in bonds and $15,000,000 in stock. The capitalization of the entire system was $21,677,933 in bonds and $25,803,947 in the stock of subsidiaries—all of which had an average guarantee of 7 per cent per annum. The Lackawanna's own stock amounted to

$25,889,000; bonds and guaranteed stocks added up to twice the stock capitalization.*

Following the end of the Civil War, the Lackawanna paid regular dividends of 10 per cent on its shares of $50 par value. It had with-stood the panic of 1873 in good shape, while railroads crashed all over the nation. But, in its very extension, it had entered into a highly competitive field, which became viciously competitive after the panic had ridden its course. It was now in trunk-line territory, bat-tling for general traffic. Cooperation, when it did appear between railroads, was slim and a cutthroat rate war was ready at any mo-ment to break out. The Lackawanna fought tooth and nail. The Erie in particular, never forgot the building of the Valley Railroad and all that it was to imply, and the Central of New Jersey, out of the hands of the receivers, well remembered John Blair's tactics which resulted in the construction of the Warren Railroad and the con-sequent loss of its own coal haul to the sea. The Lackawanna's Great Lakes outlet was at Oswego, not Buffalo, which also made it hard.

Matters were even worse in the coal business than they were in general traffic. All coal-carrying and coal-owning roads had over-extended themselves, both as carriers and as producers. There was a slack in population trends in the middle and late seventies; needed immigration fell off; the pioneers were getting their wind or resting for good on their laurels, leaving empire-building to another genera-tion. Things were quiet, winters were mild, and factories dawdled; there was more coal being dug than the market could absorb.

Gross and net earnings began to fall away on all railroads, and the Lackawanna was not to escape the general deluge. It had to sus-pend its dividends from 1876 to 1880; in the former years shares were quoted at 120 per cent of par. In 1877 they fell to a low of 30 per cent. The Lackawanna's only other period of depression had been from 1857 to 1860, when prolonged dissension among the managers, which brought about the resignation of George D. Phelps, first president, had been caused by charges of overloading in construction and land-purchase costs which, it was claimed, had diminished working capital needed to tide the road over the panic of 1857.

* Poor, *Manual of Railroads,* 1875.

President Phelps had directly charged John Blair with making a large personal profit out of right-of-way sales on the Warren Railroad. The Board of Managers held an inquiry and absolved Mr. Blair of any wrongdoing. But, just as the panic of 1857 and its aftermath brought new capital to the Lackawanna in the person of Moses Taylor, so the depression of 1873 and the ensuing oversold market of the later seventies brought into the Lackawanna fold, though briefly, one of the greatest—if not the greatest—railroad wizards of his age, in the person of Jay Gould.

A railroad, to Jay Gould, was always something on a chessboard. At the time the Lackawanna was finding itself in straitened circumstances, he was in control of the Wabash, which, with its eastern terminus at Buffalo, served as interchange for Gould's Missouri Pacific, St. Joe and Denver, Kansas Central, Katy, Texas and Pacific, Denver and Rio Grande, and the Denver, South Park and Pacific. The wizard sought a line which would pick up the Wabash business at Buffalo and carry it on down to New York. The Lackawanna, at the time no nearer to Buffalo than Binghamton, seemed a perfect pawn, if moved in the right direction. Gould bought heavily of Lackawanna stock at its then low quotation. He was on his buying spree, working as much under cover as was possible, when word of his activities came to the ears of old Moses Taylor. Nothing could be done about the stock Gould had already picked up, but Taylor went out into the market, backed by the National City Bank and his own not inconsiderable resources, and grabbed up everything still loose and in the hands of faint-hearted stockholders. He secured a controlling interest and thus checkmated Gould.

But the wizard's holdings were such that a certain deference had to be paid him and, for seven years—1881 to 1888—he served on the Board of Managers. Some historians of the Gould railroad era have referred to the Lackawanna as "a Gould property"; this was never the case, but things might have been different had Moses Taylor ever relaxed his vigilance. However, Mr. Gould must be given credit for bringing the Lackawanna into Buffalo.

Soon after he became a large stockholder, the little wizard approached Moses Taylor and his son-in-law, Percy Pyne; he sought their cooperation in building a road from Binghamton to Buffalo, there to connect with Gould's Wabash and in turn with his western

roads. Some writers hold that Gould's proposal to Moses Taylor
was born of bitterness and a desire to be avenged over the dismissal
of himself and Jim Fisk from the board of the Erie in 1872, at
which time he and Fisk had been compelled to make restitution of
$5,000,000 gathered in by Gould, Fisk, and "Boss" Tweed of New
York through fraudulent sale of Erie stock.

Be that as it may, Gould's proposal appealed to Moses Taylor,
and on August 24, 1880, articles of association were taken out for
the New York, Lackawanna and Western Railway Company. The
road was capitalized at $10,000,000 and the following directors were
chosen:

Samuel Sloan, president; John I. Blair of Blairstown;* E. S. Hig-
gins; George Bliss; Percy R. Pyne; William E. Dodge; Benjamin
G. Clarke; Jay Gould; Sidney Dillon; Russell Sage; Solon Hum-
phreys; John F. Dillon; Walter S. Gurnee.

The construction of the New York, Lackawanna and Western
was awarded to the Central Construction Company, the initial capitalization of which, set at $2,000,000, was furnished by directors of
the Lackawanna. The construction company was to be paid in mortgage bonds and in capital stock of the new road. It was a valuable
contract; indeed, it was considered so valuable by the investing
public that a few days after issuance, shares were quoted at a premium of 26 per cent. Even at that, they were impossible to pick up
—after all, it was very close to what could be termed a closed
corporation.

The road from Binghamton to Buffalo—207 miles—was well built
and quickly built. Actual cost of construction was $12,000,000, but
it was turned over to the railroad at a book value of $22,000,000, the
capitalization being $12,000,000 in 6 per cent first-mortgage bonds
and $10,000,000 in stock. One does not have to possess the acumen
of a Jay Gould to see that here was a clear profit of $10,000,000 to
the Central Construction Company stockholders participating in the
distribution of the securities.

On the completion of the New York, Lackawanna and Western,
it was offered for lease to the Wabash. That Moses Taylor or Samuel

* For some years past John Blair had been signing himself "John I. Blair of Blairstown," the name which he had given to his old home town of Gravel Hill. No
feudal baron, with his holdings recorded in the Domesday Book, had better right
to his manorial title.

Sloan, president of the new road as well as of the Lackawanna, ever intended the Wabash to get hold seems absurd; what Jay Gould had in mind as to its disposal was most likely upset by the sudden financial bogging-down of the Wabash. Edging to eventual receivership, the Wabash could take on no further commitments. Neither Moses Taylor nor Samuel Sloan could have been displeased, although Mr. Taylor's pleasure was short-lived; he died in April, 1882.

At a meeting of the Board of Managers of the Lackawanna, held at 26 Exchange Place, New York, on September 29, 1882, a perpetual lease was approved between the Lackawanna and the New York, Lackawanna and Western Railway Company, by which the Lackawanna obligated itself to an annual payment of 5 per cent on $10,000,000 of capital stock and guaranteed the $12,000,000 worth of bonds. A similar leasing arrangement had been made with the New York, Lackawanna and Western Railway Company of Pennsylvania, formed to give the line state protection where it jutted into Pennsylvania between the border towns of Barton and Chemung.

The Lackawanna was now a through line from Buffalo to New York, but minority stockholders objected to the deal. The $10,000,-000 of capital stock on which 5 per cent had been guaranteed was clear profit for the Central Construction Company stockholders; in addition to that, the mortgage bonds were selling at a premium. A group of minority stockholders went into court, claiming that they had a prior right to subscribe to the construction-company securities. Their plea was denied.

The Lackawanna was now in fine position to go after trunk-line business, and the trunk-line pool was functioning. But President Sloan wanted to try out as a lone wolf, at any rate for a little while, so that he could watch how the wind blew. He made an alliance with the Grand Trunk, whereby the latter got its full proportion of through rates to the West, even though the rate quoted on the Lackawanna was reduced. Wholesale cutting of rates was accomplished by reducing the classification of a long list of commodities. As the coal business, to which prosperity had returned, was now giving the Lackawanna a good basis for profitable operation, the line appeared to be in a position to carry the fight to the limit without endangering its solvency, while threatening the existence of the trunk-line pool.

The difficulties of the pool had been further increased by another lone wolf, the New York, West Shore and Buffalo Railroad, built from New York to Buffalo as competition to the New York Central. Finally, the Lackwanna was induced to enter the pool—not the least-considered portion of the general inducement being the bankruptcy of the New York, West Shore and Buffalo. The agreement was signed November 14, 1884, by the Baltimore and Ohio, the Grand Trunk of Canada, the New York, West Shore, and Buffalo (in receivership), the New York Central, the Pennsylvania, the Erie, and the Lackawanna. Mr. Sloan's road was to get 12.6 per cent of the west-bound business.

The Lackawanna began steady and ever-increasing traffic with the West, doing most of its interchange with the Grand Trunk and the Wabash. But the hauling of its own coal over its own tracks was to remain its major occupation until the overflowing population of New York City spread into New Jersey and became commuters.

12 *Refurbishing Job*

DURING the eighties the cost of everything went up in these United States—labor, material, bread, and housing. Previous living standards, as among the working classes, had not been so greatly different in the New World from those obtaining in the Old World. The railroad and labor riots which so seriously affected the trunk lines between the Atlantic seaboard and the western states began July 16, 1877, when the Baltimore and Ohio ordered a 10 per cent wage cut. The terror of the Molly Maguires, the killings and the burnings, are badly blotted pages in the histories of both management and labor, and the Lackawanna was in the thick of things.

Big business throughout the nation had come to realize, without union prodding, that wages were pitifully inadequate. Wages went up. As a result, you might say that in the early eighties was inaugurated, with best intentions, that vicious cycle which—better illustrated today than in any other period of our history—jumps a man's salary, jumps his rent, jumps the price of steak, jumps the cost of a loaf of bread, so that, in the end, his pocket is just as empty as it ever was.

In 1881, at peace with its help, but with tough competition all around, the Lackawanna found its operating ratio cost on the rise. For that year it was not bad, 49.81 per cent. But for 1882 it went to 61.35 per cent. This was brought down, in 1883, to 58.03 per cent, still high. Sam Sloan decided to quit playing lone wolf, made

peace with the pool, and became a part of it. The year 1885 marked
the beginning of a boom, and the trunk-line harmony brought the
Lackawanna's operating ratio down to 52.73. Freight ton-mileage
shot up from 676,211,610 for 1881 to 1,315,249,598 for 1886.

In 1883 Mr. Sloan inaugurated a policy of paying for improvements out of current income and charging the cost to the yearly
income. In 1883 there was appropriated for renewal $982,500 from
income; in 1884 this appropriation amounted to $131,253.84. These
were the expenditure totals, and it became a bookkeeping practice
to charge expenditures for renewals and betterments to a suspense
account, cleared annually or semiannually by charging the amount
against income, instead of crediting it to the investment account
and thus building up the latter.

The eighties also saw the emergence of the Lackawanna into
what was to become a strategic position in the suburban area of
northern New Jersey, concerning which more will be told later.
The road was no longer just a coal carrier. The change in gross
earnings is best illustrated by figures from annual reports:

	1882	1886	1890
Passenger	$2,278,607	$3,028,487	$4,146,185
General Freight	$3,082,399	$5,611,691	$7,173,398
Coal	$7,117,853	$9,035,664	$9,799,440

In 1890 the Standard Oil Company gained control of the Lackawanna's fiscal adjutant, the National City Bank. Proof was again
forthcoming that over the years the railroad has always been fortunate in attracting to membership on its Board of Managers (Directors) outstanding figures in finance and industry. The Rockefellers
and Rockefeller associates began to make their appearance on the
board after acquisition of the bank. William (John D's. brother)
took his seat at the February meeting in 1890 and remained a director for thirty-one years until his retirement in December, 1921. John
D. Rockefeller, Jr., served from 1898 to 1914.

One of the most potent influences in the latter-day development
of the Lackawanna was George Fisher Baker, who served on the
board from February, 1892, until December, 1921.

Upon the occasion of the resignation from the board of Messrs.
William Rockefeller and George F. Baker Sr., in December, 1921, in

fulfillment of the requirements of an order of the Interstate Commerce Commission, the following appears in the minutes:

"That we should be deprived of the sound judgment, mature experience and intimate knowledge of its affairs, so abundantly possessed by these two members of our Board, we feel assured, an irretrievable misfortune not only to the Company but to the public at large."

Pursuant to the same order Harold S. Vanderbilt resigned, after having been on the board from February, 1913, and concerning him the following appears in the minutes:

"We had hoped to have the benefit of his advice for many years, and believe his forced retirement a distinct loss to the Company."

In the decade from 1881 to 1890 coal tonnage increased 32 per cent, general freight business 160 per cent, and passenger traffic 88 per cent. This last increase, ever rising, was and is almost wholly New Jersey–New York commutation, fed by the Lackawanna to the Hoboken ferries plying across the Hudson. This flow, to and fro, of passenger traffic growing by leaps and bounds finally resulted in the taking over by the Lackawanna of the Hoboken Ferry Company.

Coal property operations continued to yield a profit in certain years, despite periodic overproduction and keen competition. The record over this decade is particularly satisfactory when compared with other railroad-owned coal properties, which are uniformly reporting large losses. The Lackawanna was paying a regular dividend of 7 per cent, and stock was quoted at a large premium above par.*

In 1892, under the presidency of Archibald A. McLeod, the Philadelphia and Reading Railroad sought to form a combine of all anthracite and northern New England systems into a monopoly. The plan was financed by Vanderbilt and Morgan interests, spearheaded by William K. Vanderbilt, who represented his family's interests in control of the New York Central and in the operation of the Michigan Central, the Chicago and North Western, and half a dozen other lines. Despite large stock purchases in the Delaware and Hudson, the Lehigh Valley, the New Jersey Central, and the Pennsylvania, "the Reading operation" failed to accomplish its pur-

* Bogen, John I., *History of the Anthracite Railroads,* The Macmillan Company, New York.

pose. Vanderbilt had also obtained 40,000 shares of Lackawanna stock and an armful of proxies, but, even with a purchase of another 40,000 shares, he was unable to wrest control from the Rockefellers and the National City Bank.

When "the Reading operation" collapsed, the Vanderbilt-Morgan interests held a 15 per cent interest in the Lackawanna. Frederick W. Vanderbilt appeared on the board, as of February, 1895, and served until his retirement, February, 1916. Harold S. Vanderbilt was elected February, 1913, and served until December, 1921. The interest acquired by the Vanderbilts and Morgans did not alter in any way the smoothness of the Lackawanna operation, but the stock acquisition did give the Vanderbilt-owned New York Central a voice in the operation of every railroad in the State of New York except the Erie.

In March, 1899, Samuel Sloan retired from the presidency of the Lackawanna, full of years and of honors. He had been at the helm for just five months short of thirty-two years, and he had brought his ship through stormy waters to a safe and sound financial anchorage. He had fought his way to victory through the bitterness of the anthracite competition, through the even greater bitterness of the trunk-line rate wars. Under his guidance the Lackawanna had successfully survived without reorganization, when most of the coal roads had in turn been forced through bankruptcy, receivership, successful—and unsuccessful—reorganization.

Mr. Sloan was succeeded by William Haynes Truesdale, at the time first vice-president and general manager of the Chicago, Rock Island and Pacific. Like Sloan he had come up from the ranks, entering railroad service as a clerk following graduation from Rock Island, Illinois, High School. Immediately upon assuming office Mr. Truesdale threw away an ancient Lackawanna fetish—one that might have caused considerable trouble and dissension, had not substantial dividends been always forthcoming. This was the policy of secrecy in the annual reports, which, while giving capital figures, disdained to inform the general public regarding details.

The 1899 report issued by President Truesdale, the first full report since the panic of 1857, was a frank document, laying before both the investor and the man-on-the-street salient facts about the Lackawanna which constituted a warning, instead of proffering the usual yearly pat on the back accompanied by a dividend check. Mr. Truesdale pointed out that for some time lower rail rates had been forced on the roads; that earning power would have to be increased if 7 per cent checks were to be the continued order of the day. Mr. Truesdale laid it down that there would have to be much-needed improvements all over the right-of-way in order to bring the property into really first-class condition.

The Lackawanna had gone along for years with many difficult grades, ancient bridges built to avoid fills and embankments, and sharp curves which needed ironing out. Such make-do's had served their purpose when the Lackawanna was nothing more than a coal carrier. Coal, as Mr. Truesdale impressed upon his stockholders, did not mind being bumped around, but Class A traffic, in the form of sometimes captious patrons, was wont to object. Too much bumping, went on the president, was likely to send people to other lines. There was now no lack of competition, both freight and passenger, in Lackawanna territory.

The new president was determined to modernize the road thoroughly. And he was the right man for the job. He had come to the Lackawanna fresh from a major bridge-building job for the Rock Island, which had been hitting into more sparsely populated and untamed areas in the Middle West and Far West than any other American railroad. He had negotiated canyons, circled mountains or dug through them, and had adequately spanned waters which in summer were trickles of damp sand, but which in winter became raging torrents. The man who had truss-tamed the Red River, the Cimmarron, and the Canadian was surely qualified to deal with the Hackensack, the Passaic, and even the Delaware.

Bridge construction and renovation was the biggest refurbishing job. Over a period of three years the Lackawanna spent $3,700,000 on this item alone. For organization purposes the main line had been divided into three divisions: the Morris and Essex, the Scranton, and the Buffalo. Over the Morris and Essex the ruling grade was reduced to 45 feet per mile; on the Scranton division this was cut to 50 to 78 feet per mile for lengths of 18 miles; and on the Buffalo division working grades of 20 feet were the rule, with one section of 8 miles having a 60-foot grade. The work called for many fills

PHOEBE SNOW

(from the original painting by Penrhyn Stanlaus)

Tablet to Madison's (New Jersey) first train

The "Essex," which pulled the train—1837

SPITFIRE

Built in England in 1838.   Bought by D., L. & W. R. R. Co. in 1851.
The Company's first locomotive.

"Spitfire" in its later years, banished to a log dump

The "Waterloo," which hauled Morris and Essex passengers from 1864 to 1894

The "Stanhope," Morris and Essex woodburner, which operated on that sort of power from 1864 to 1892

The "Madison" (D. L. and W. No. 24). Engineer George ("Lopear") Nicholas—in the cab—said she "could run like a frightened deer"—1864 to 1874

The "Jennie" of the Morris and Essex, 1867 to 1891

The "Luther Wright" (Oswego and Syracuse Railroad). Pride of the Eighties

Old "Twenty-Two" and crew take on a little glamour

The Boonton Local—summer, 1895

Selden Scranton

George W. Scranton

Samuel Sloan

William H. Truesdale

John M. Davis

Wm. White

The Tunkhannock Viaduct

"The Lackawanna Valley," painted by George Inness. Gifted to the National Gallery of Art by Mrs. Huddleston Rogers. Inness was commissioned for this picture by George D. Phelps, first president of the Lackawanna

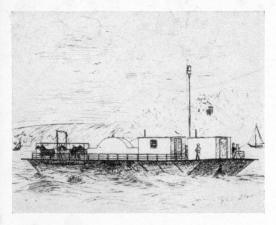

Hoboken Ferry "Team Boat." Circa 1800

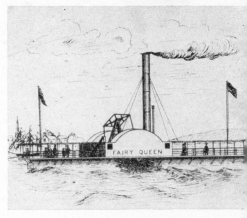

The "Fairy Queen," 1827

The "Binghamton"

Lackawanna Freight Terminal, Jersey City, New Jersey

The Lackawanna Limited roars over a bridge

The "Phoebe Snow." Lackawanna streamliner—New York to Buffalo

and tunnels. The roadbed was reballasted throughout, and most of the line was relaid with 80-pound rails.*

Another feature of Mr. Truesdale's reconstruction program was extensive terminal and equipment improvements. As traffic increased, it became necessary to develop new facilities in the congested New York Harbor district. The Lackawanna Terminal was reorganized along simple but efficient lines. The Hoboken waterfront setup was extended to a length of about half a mile along the river front to join the Erie at Jersey City, and a four-track line was built through the Bergen Hill tunnel. In the year 1903 alone, 150 new powerful locomotives were placed in service. In the report for that year the company showed two locomotives for every three miles of track and thirty cars for every mile of operated track.†

The Lackawanna's biggest engineering feat—not during this reconstruction period, but in its entire history—was the building of its cutoff from Slateford, Pennsylvania, to Port Morris, New Jersey. This was begun in 1908, the object being to shorten the distance to Buffalo by 11 miles, as well as to eliminate a number of steep grades and difficult curves on the most congested portion of the line, a section of most irregular topography. ‡ Credit for this tremendous job belongs to Lincoln Bush and G. J. Ray.

In 1908 the Lackawanna Railroad Company of New Jersey was organized to finance the building of a direct, low-grade line over this 24⁸⁄₁₀-mile stretch, the cost being a little over $11,000,000. This outlay was covered by capital stock given to the Lackawanna, which guaranteed 4 per cent dividends, distributed to stockholders as a special 35 per cent dividend. Another cutoff was built in 1912–1915, from Clark's Summit to Hallstead, Pennsylvania. This job was financed by the sale of $12,000,000 of new stock to shareholders at par—$50—although its market value, on December 12, 1912, went as high as $298. At this time all stock prices were quoted on the basis of $100 par value, so that the investor's market value reached $597 for $100 par value.

* White, William, *Modernizing a Trunk Line—The Lackawanna Railroad.* (*Note.* This William White, a compiler and publisher of business brochures during the early nineteen hundreds, is not to be confused with William White, present president of the Lackawanna.)
† *Railway World*, Vol. 29.
‡ Delaware, Lackawanna and Western, *Annual Report*, 1907.

This tremendous modernizing job went into maintenance-of-way cost and shot up the operating ratio. Additions and betterments for 1901 had run up a total of $1,228,953. In 1902 this was figured at $1,632,737. In 1903 it was $1,478,106. But the surplus grew steadily, and after 1902 the coal business again bounded away up. In 1903 this department set up a new record, earning $3,036,194, and did not go below this figure for twenty years. Special reserves, set aside for railroad renewals and betterments, never amounted to less than $1,000,000 from 1901 to the outbreak of the First World War. In 1906 this amounted to $5,551,619. From 1901 to 1914, a total of $40,839,716 was set aside for this purpose.

Anthracite coal, the digging, hauling, and selling of which brought the Lackawanna into being, is not as important a revenue getter for the line as it was in the early days, but it is still the major prop of its transportation business. Divested of its coal properties by the government in 1921, with a ruling that a coal owner could not be a coal hauler and vice versa, the Lackawanna turned the coal-owning interests over to the Glen Alden Coal Company.

In 1948 the Lackawanna moved a total of 6,669,526 net tons of anthracite coal, producing revenue of $12,759,633; this was the largest single commodity handled, as to both tonnage and revenue. Bituminous-coal haulage is also an important revenue source. In 1948 the road carried 4,635,050 tons of bituminous coal, bringing in $4,347,573. Shorter haul for the bituminous product explains the difference between the soft-coal and hard-coal revenue, although the former was 70 per cent of the latter. In 1899 only 349,563 tons of bituminous coal were moved; in 1923 the total reached 2,620,977 tons and almost doubled a quarter of a century later.

The development of this railroad of less than a thousand miles in length is an amazing tribute to its founders and its developers. Out of William Henry's dream of digging coal and hauling it to market over those new-fangled strap rails came realization through practical George Scranton, who bought the coal land, dug the anthracite, forged T rail, and laid track.

Through John Blair came extension from the coal regions to the sea. Through Moses Taylor came further expansion and protection of the Lackawanna's good name by fending off and outwitting the railroad robber barons. In the hands of Samuel Sloan, a simple coal carrier became a major trunk line and, as such, also a means of transport to pleasant suburban homes for weary New Yorkers. The Lackawanna marched ever forward under Mr. Truesdale's successor, John M. Davis, who had risen from stenographer in a railroad office to a vice-presidency of the Baltimore and Ohio. The march ahead continues under William White, who succeeded Mr. Davis in 1941, coming up from the ranks as have come all Lackawanna presidents since the days of Sam Sloan.

Taken by and large and with reference to present lifetimes, the stockholders of the Lackawanna have been lucky, though these are difficult days for all railroads. In 1904 an extra dividend of 10 per cent was paid, in addition to the regular 7 per cent rate. In 1905 dividend payments totaled 19¼ per cent. In 1906 a policy was established of paying a 10 per cent dividend over and above the regular 10 per cent dividend. In July, 1909, an extra cash dividend of 50 per cent was declared, one half of which was used to buy stock in the Delaware, Lackawanna and Western Coal Company, scheduled to take over the marketing activities of the road's coal department. The coal company offered stock at par—fifty dollars—to Lackawanna stockholders, and this sold from the start at a large premium in the open market. As if this were not enough, a stock dividend of 15 per cent was paid from new shares in an intercompany merger.

When the Glen Alden Company was formed to take over the Lackawanna's coal interests, owners of railroad shares bought Glen Alden stock at $5, and in a short time it was quoted on the open market at $150. On top of this came a payment of a 100 per cent stock dividend on acceptance by the road of the provisions of the Pennsylvania Constitution as regards charters. The old special charter had forbidden stock dividends.

After 1931 the Lackawanna paid no dividends until 1948 when a twenty-five-cent dividend was declared. This was repeated in 1949.

Part II: THE MEN WHO MADE THE RAILROAD

13   *The Fearless Amateurs*

As you look into the origins of a railroad—almost any railroad—you know pretty well what you are going to find. Nowadays there are not many doom shouters left to deny that the railroads, with magnificent disdain for geography and political frontiers, made the country. It is only natural that the men who made the railroads should have been a breed that respected few barriers. There were giants in those days because there had to be.

They came from no particular walk of life or social stratum. Some started out wealthy. Some did not. One in a hundred of them had enough mechanical background to tell the difference between a link motion and a spark arrester. Few of them knew how a steam locomotive worked—or cared. But they were alike in at least two respects: All of them knew the necessity for a closer connection between goods and markets. All of them had horizons beyond the next hill.

They were all men who had had experience supplying the needs of others—merchants of dry goods and groceries, tea and sugar importers, founders, cattlemen, shipowners, mining men. They were producers unable to get their wares to the consumer in the seaboard settlements. They were merchandisers in the coastal strip (which was virtually all of America) who would get a stock of goods more readily from England than from, say, Slocum's Hollow. In the beginning only a few of them—the bankers, who had learned something about the profits of the transportation business from the Erie Canal—were interested in the money-making possibilities of the railroads.

What the majority wanted was some means of getting things from *there* to *here*, even if they had to build it themselves.

At the beginning of the nineteenth century, seventeen years after the Revolutionary War, the United States was by no means the benighted community most Americans seem to think it was. It had been quick to alter its colonial position as a raw material supply depot for Britain. Factories were becoming a part of the landscape all along the Atlantic. The millinery business was resurgent. And new houses, in the cities at least, were being built with more attention to comfort. But at the same time, the country was still too close to the edge of the wilderness to let its people get very soft. Only a few miles from the principal settlements everybody was a pioneer or the son of a pioneer. The uncooperative Indians still wandered around in the woods. And if people of the rural populations did not know how to make things for themselves, they went without. The railroad builders came largely from that sort of stock.

They were basically tough. They took good fortune as it came. They were not surprised at adversity. They did not ask for quarter, and, it must be admitted, a lot of them did not give any. After training in a world where actual cash was little more than hearsay, they were universally canny about wasting a dollar. But they were willing to risk fortunes on what they believed in, just as, not so long before, they would have risked their lives. Most of them were Scotch, English, or Northern Irish, presumably because the bulk of the people in New York City were Scotch, English, or Northern Irish. That most of them were likewise Presbyterian goes without saying.

As we see them in their portraits, they appear to have been a stately group. With their tall beaver hats, frock coats, tight trousers, frilled shirts, fawn-colored waistcoats, heavy gold watch chains, high collars, and bow ties, one of them looks quite like another. They were all strong-jawed, eagle-eyed, beetle-browed, and stern.

You wonder, as you lay down the old photograph album, if any of these men ever found anything worth smiling at. It seems unlikely. Life was real, life was earnest, a hundred years ago, and the jokers do not seem to have got very far.

It is significant, however, that few of them showed one character in business and another in private. Whatever they were, they were. When Sam Sloan halted traffic on the Lackawanna on Sundays (at a considerable loss in revenue) it was because he had a different but consistent idea of what constituted right and wrong. Many of these men endowed colleges and supported other philanthropies which keep their names alive today, long after their connection with America's transportation has been forgotten. And the majority of them lived without scandal and died without scandal. While many of them may have been difficult to live with, they must have had their special endowments. They did a good job of railroad building.

14 *Tumult and Shouting*

Two branches of the Phelps family, somewhat distantly related, helped make the early history of the Ligett's Gap Railroad and attended its metamorphosis through the Cobb's Gap merger into the Delaware, Lackawanna and Western. If you go back far enough, you find that they both sprang from the family of John Phelps, who was secretary to Oliver Cromwell, Lord Protector of England and nemesis of King Charles I. The brothers who founded the two lines came to Connecticut Colony in 1650.

In the story of the Lackawanna, the original Phelps was Anson, the metals broker, and father-in-law of William Earle Dodge, his partner. Associated with him, but not too closely, in this unfamiliar undertaking, were a couple of merchants who belonged to the other side of his family, John Jay and George D. Phelps. One of this pair, John Jay, seems to have been the typical successful business-man of his time. His brother, George, who may have led a sheltered life somewhere before he got pushed into the railroad business, was a highly literate and extremely vocal man, whose previous experience had not encompassed anything like John Insley Blair. He is unique among the financiers of the 1850's in that he is remembered prin-cipally for his conscience.

Perhaps it is wrong to say that the affairs of the Lackawanna just before the Civil War were conducted under guidance from on high. But there is no doubt whatever that many of the directors were convinced of their heavenly appointment. One finds evidence of this touching faith in the minutes of the years 1853 to 1858, which give the impression that the railroad for that period was operated as the joint enterprise of the company's Board of Managers and the good-conduct committee of the Presbyterian Church.

Were it not for this mandate and a brief connection with the railroad, the name of George D. Phelps might be forgotten today. But the business of running a railroad according to high ethical standards seems to have been something to which he could put his mind.

He was elected to the Board of Managers in January, 1853, succeeded his brother John Jay as president in February, 1853, holding this office until September, 1856, and continued to make the operational policies of the company a matter of public interest, if not amusement.

On the Board of Managers at the same time was William Earle Dodge, whose advance to the Scrantons for iron rails in 1846 provided the first excuse for the construction of the line from Scranton to the Susquehanna. He was likewise Mr. Phelps's next-door neighbor, which may have had something to do with subsequent developments.

Mr. Dodge seems to have been a firmly upstanding sort of man who, like so many early Covenanters engaged in business in those days, took a leading part in reform movements. Some of his leanings may have come from his father-in-law and partner, Anson G. Phelps, who had been brought up as the ward of a minister. But Dodge's own opinions on human behavior probably did not need much encouragement. He was an early follower of John B. Gough and Father Matthew in the cause of temperance, and from 1865 until his death in 1883 he was president of the National Temperance Society. He had advanced views on war and its futility, and as a Republican member of Congress from New York City in 1866, fought somewhat unsuccessfully for a moderate policy in the Reconstruction. He was a man of pleasant manners and a fine physical presence.

However, he did allow his coachman or somebody to dump coal and other things in Mr. George Phelps's carriageway which adjoined his own. Therefore, on October 5, 1854, Mr. Phelps wrote to Mr. Dodge, apologizing for having to write.

My present object is to . . . express my unfeigned regret at the necessity for pursuing a course so repugnant to all my feelings. My interests at stake in the possible depreciation of my property are large. If I have any legal redress, it is my duty to seek it. If I have none, I will endeavor patiently to bear the wrongs for which I can find no relief. Sincerely desiring a continuance of our former kind relations, I remain . . .

Phelps carried this letter around in his pocket for a week and then added a postscript.

My last week's experience has not left me a ray of hope for any relief. . . . For two days or more [you] have kept the alley blocked up and impassable with your coal. On Saturday I could not get my carriage out of my stable and was obliged to forego its use. On Sunday it was only got out by hauling it over and through your heaps of coal.

Dodge replied that perhaps it would be just as well to let the law decide the rights of the matter, and Phelps got an injunction. On January 26, 1855, Dodge, who may have needed some more coal, wrote to Phelps urging him to drop the contest in a spirit of Christian brotherhood. Phelps agreed, with certain qualifications. Then there were more disagreements and more lawsuits, and in November, 1856, Phelps sold his house and moved away. All of these proceedings were on the friendliest basis. As Mr. Phelps afterward testified, "Within a month past, Mr. Dodge has voluntarily and with great satisfaction to me, occupied a seat in my pew at church on the Sabbath."

Phelps's policies in office as president of the road were novel enough to be unthinkable. He objected to the accepted practices of buying coal from a company subsidiary for less than market price and of paying rebates to the subsidiary coal company on freight charges for coal carried by the railroad. In this, of course, he was only following the line of thought taken by the government about fifty years later, but he was certainly an unpopular agitator. He was one of a breed, once more numerous than now, which had the strength of its convictions.

It took him a little time to make up his mind what he was going to do about it. He turned in his resignation, gave the matter some further thought, and then withdrew it.

In 1856, after an uneventful year of routine business, Mr. Phelps got a new idea. He recommended that the bylaws be revised to permit the appointment of an auditor. This time his fellow managers looked at him in open amazement that bordered on suspicion. Such arrant waste of company funds had never been heard of before— at any rate, not in a railroad office.

The board, as part of a routine procedure, appointed a committee to consider what, if anything, an auditor might be used for. The committee consisted of Manager Henry Young and Manager John I. Blair.

On August 26, 1856, Messrs. Young and Blair returned an unfavorable report on Phelps's recommendation. On September 9, 1856, Mr. Phelps issued a statement to the stockholders accompanied by another resignation. It was accepted.

One might think that Mr. Phelps would have welcomed the time and opportunity thus given him to carry on his row with Mr. Dodge. But it seems that he was not yet through with the affairs of the Lackawanna. Whatever else you may say of him, he had a keen sense of his duty to make others see things as he saw them. In January, 1857, he sent around a second letter to the stockholders.

This appears to have changed the attitude of his one-time associates on the board from annoyance to resentment; for, a month later, it was resolved:

That officers of this company be instructed to furnish the said Phelps no copies or statements, whatever, touching the affairs or business of the company, publication by said Phelps in the month of December last of a certain pamphlet having disclosed copies of various confidential papers of the company improperly contained by him.

An investigating committee, two members of which were named by Phelps, was appointed by the committee of stockholders on March 3, under the chairmanship of Christopher R. Robert, a deeply religious man who succeeded George Phelps in the presidency of the road. Robert, descendant of French Huguenots, had come to the East via New Orleans and Galena, Illinois, and had acquired a fortune and a senior partnership in a firm importing tea and sugar. He is remembered today chiefly for his founding of Robert College in Constantinople, which has trained many of the leaders in the nations of the Middle East and is generally regarded as one of America's most successful cultural outposts. He was superintendent of the Sunday school and an elder of the Laight Street Presbyterian Church, New York City, for nearly thirty years.

Nothing much came of the investigation except bitter words in polite language, for most of the committee members had their own versions of what was right and were just as stubborn as George Phelps. The minutes show that various communications were received by the Board of Managers from the recent president; they seem to have been ignored. Mr. Phelps eventually subsided, and contemporary biographers wot not of him until the end of the year, when he brought out the first of a series of pamphlets, "Corporate Abuses and Ecclesiastical Absurdities," bearing the imprint "John A. Gray and Green, Printers, Stereotypers and Binders; *Fireproof Buildings*, Corner of Frankfort and Jacob Streets, New York."

The initial pamphlet bore the subtitle: "History of the Recent Investigation Into the Affairs of the Delaware, Lackawanna, and Western Railroad Company; with remarks upon the report of the committee designed to disabuse the minds of the stockholders, and, at the same time, to show the doubtful benefit, if not the positive evils of such investigations and the unfairness of this one in particular."

Mr. Phelps was thorough. He opened with the investigating committee's alleged finding that he had shown a "vindictiveness toward Mr. Dodge rarely seen in a man of sound mind"—a charge which, incidentally, the investigating committee had never made. And he answered it by printing his correspondence relative to the blocked alley.

He was bitter about Blair because, he said, Blair had taken a $200 bonus for making a loan of $10,000 to the company. There was a fine to-do about that.

The payment of a 5 per cent extra commission as a sort of bonus to managers who would endorse company acceptances was legal, he wrote. It had been authorized by the Board of Managers. But he contended that Blair had agreed to put up the $10,000 at 8 per cent without any extra commission and had collected the $200 through subterfuge. He had made Blair give it back. But that had not ended the transaction—not when it was a transaction involving as much as $200 and Blair. The genial squire of Blairstown put in another claim and received another check.

Phelps had other things to say about coal contracts, and the suggestion that Blair had tinkered with locomotives to their detriment. He mentioned that at the time of his resignation the floating debt of the company had been counterbalanced by assets on hand. And there for a time, he rested. The report of the investigating committee became the most popular summer reading in New York. It showed no friendliness for Mr. Phelps.

It was the opinion of the committee that Mr. Phelps's various charges were not so. Discussion dragged along while the one-time president was getting out some new books in his series, and everybody was willing to forget the whole business when, along toward the end of 1859, he dumped the whole matter into the lap of the Presbyterian Church.

This was probably the only time in American history when a church was asked to go into matters having to do even indirectly with the management of a railroad.

In this instance, the only member of the railroad Board of Managers who was a member of Mr. Phelps's church, where the proceedings had to originate, was the long-suffering William E. Dodge. And in many ways Mr. Dodge seemed made to order.

Phelps began with a plea to Dodge, for whom he seems to have always entertained a sneaking regard. But Mr. Dodge does not seem to have been willing to turn the other cheek. After an interchange of correspondence, only one side of which (Mr. Phelps's) has come down to us, Mr. Phelps tapped him to represent the Lackawanna Board of Managers before a session of the Madison Square Presbyterian Church, in subsequent hearings before the Fourth Presbytery of New York, and, finally, on appeal, to the Synod of New York and New Jersey.

These amazing proceedings went on through 1862 and part of 1863, sharing attention with the campaign in Maryland, the Battle of Shiloh, and the Battle of Gettysburg. But Mr. Phelps does not seem to have made much headway. Toward the end, the various boards of inquiry seem to have grown deaf to argument.

The finding of the Session was "that in view of all the circumstances of the case, and in the exercise of the discretion enjoined upon the Session in our book of discipline, it is inexpedient for the Session to entertain the charges and specifications of Mr. Phelps against Mr. Dodge, and that the same are hereby dismissed. . . . Resolved that the clerk communicate foregoing to Mr. Phelps."

Action by the Presbytery was more brief. An appeal from the opinion of the Session was denied. Phelps was willing to give up then, as well he might have been—but by that time publicity given the wrangle attracted the attention of the Synod of New York and New Jersey. The Synod seems to have dumped all the charges having to do with the Lackawanna board meeting and to have considered merely whether or not Mr. Dodge had been unkind to Mr. Phelps. The committee reviewing this phase of the case eventually recommended "no correction of the action of Presbytery." William Earle Dodge and, by association, the other managers of the Lackawanna were definitely vindicated.

After the publication of "Corporate Abuses and Ecclesiastical Absurdities" Mr. Phelps kept up his campaign with "letters to the editor" all over the United States until his death in the eighties. The Lackawanna, unsanctified but uncondemned, has continued on its nonecclesiastical way.

15 *Better Mousetraps*

CONSIDERING the career of Samuel Sloan, who ran the Lackawanna for thirty-two years, you reach the conclusion that a man who can build a better mousetrap can also make a better something else. Sloan, unlike many associated with him on the Board of Managers, had little personal interest in better transportation. He was an importer and commission merchant and had made a comfortable fortune in his line before he ever had a ride on a steam train. It had made no difference to him whether produce from the middle of Pennsylvania or upper New York got to the New York market late—or at all. The stocks he sold would continue to be available as long as ships should sail the Atlantic. He had dabbled a bit in Brooklyn real estate, also with success. And with that preparation, he became a railroad president, and a good one.

Samuel Sloan was born in Northern Ireland, near Belfast, in December, 1817, and was brought to New York by his parents when a year old. The sudden death of his father in 1831 brought an end to his formal schooling. He was fourteen years old and a student at Columbia College Preparatory School, but he had to turn to and help support a family of five children. His first two years in the employ of a merchant who had a working schedule of fifteen hours a day were described by him later as "difficult." But, characteristically, he recalled the time between his sixteenth and twenty-first birthdays as the most important years of his life. His father had left him two pieces of advice, "choose only good men for friends and read only good books." Young Sam remembered. In 1833 he went to work for the linen-importing firm of McBride and Company, became a member of the Mercantile Library Association, and began to look about for the friends his father had described. He had a young manhood well filled with hard work.

His mother's health began to fail in the second year of her widowhood, and presently the boy found himself, not only provider for his brothers and sisters, but adviser in matters of education, religion, even love and matrimony. The family survived the Asiatic cholera epidemic of 1832, which killed 2,998 people in three months and virtually depopulated New York. Samuel came unscathed through the abolitionist riots of 1834, which ebbed and flowed repeatedly around the premises of McBride and Company. In 1835 he narrowly escaped with his life while saving the company records from the fire that burned out most of the buildings between Wall, William, and Fulton Streets on the East River. But, on the whole, his routine in the linen business could hardly be called spectacular until he was made a partner of McBride and Company in 1844. He was then twenty-seven. That same year he married Margaret Elmendorf at her father's house in New Brunswick, New Jersey.

It would be unjust to say that Samuel Sloan lived obscurely for the first thirty-seven years of his life. During that time he had become virtually head of an importing concern that had weathered two major financial panics. He was known personally to most of the important merchants and professional men in New York. And there is no doubt that he was well liked. The Ulsterman's wit and the Sloan personality gave him an unusual position in a serious world.

He first became interested in railroads because he foresaw the part they must play in opening up the wilderness beyond the mountains. He knew them for what they were, the toys of a lot of eager woodcutters, blacksmiths, miners, and farmers, unqualified to deal with anybody's problems but their own. Nevertheless, he invested heavily in rail securities. Steam transportation had to come, he was convinced, and not even waste and inefficiency could hold it back.

In 1855 he had enough holdings in the Hudson River Railroad— one day to become a part of the New York Central system—to get himself elected to the board of directors. Shortly afterward he was elected president. Then he set about the painful business of learning how to run a railroad.

He was helped a little by the fact that all the railroads in the country in that period were still in an experimental stage, and he probably knew as much about them as anybody else. But, considering his later performance, one is prompted to give him plenty of credit for natural aptitude.

Poor's *History of the Railroads of the United States* (New York, 1860) gives an amazing picture of how high hopes and catastrophic losses were so frequently linked in those early projects. Fifty railroads had been incorporated in New York State before 1860. Of these more than four-fifths had gone into bankruptcy. The Hudson River line was better off than most, because it had a right-of-way through a productive and fairly populous territory and connected two cities, New York and Albany, that had good reason for being connected. But even as Sloan took his seat on the board of directors, the road began to have the same sort of troubles that plagued less favored routes. For one thing the management was having great difficulty finding money with which to meet the interest on bonded indebtedness. And there, of course, was a fine opportunity for Mr. Sloan. He may not have known anything about railroads, but he did know plenty about how to raise money.

His biography, written by his son-in-law, Joseph Rankin Duryee,* says that he put his money into the Hudson River Railroad because he had faith in the board of directors. And this is most likely true. He also had faith in Sam Sloan. It was one of his axioms that *things* are not good or bad except as *men* make them so. And there were a lot of his well-chosen cronies on the board of the Hudson River line.

He learned the mechanics of railroad operation by getting out on the right-of-way with the engineers and switchmen and station agents and trackwalkers—something few railroad presidents had ever done before him. John M. Toucey, one-time passenger agent of the road, said later that Sam Sloan knew every employee on the payroll, in the offices and on the trains, and that he got what he

* DURYEE, JOSEPH RANKIN, *The Story of Samuel and Margaret Sloan*, New York, 1927.

wanted out of all of them through an inborn gift of leadership.

He was definitely a progressive. He was the first railroad executive in the country to arrange for the use of the Morse telegraph in running trains. He was quick to advocate good roadbeds and heavy rail. One of his first official acts was to lease a line into Troy, because it would give the Hudson River line freight and passenger business to the north, east, and west. During his term as president the stock of the road rose from $17 to $140 a share.

In 1858 Cornelius Vanderbilt got control of the Hudson River line and put in a new board of directors. Sloan was offered the presidency of Vanderbilt's Harlem Railroad with flattering inducements. But he declined.

"Commodore," he said, "you and I can't each be the sole boss of the same job and work together." And the Commodore replied, "Sam, you're right."

Sloan resigned from the presidency of the Hudson River road to put in two years as arbitrator and commissioner of the trunk lines —the Erie, Pennsylvania, Baltimore and Ohio, and New York Central systems—which, until 1865, had operated on a policy of dog-eat-dog. During the same years he formed a connection with the National City Bank and the Farmers Loan and Trust Company. He became a director of both. It is probably significant that the president and chief stockholder of the National City Bank was his intimate friend, Moses Taylor, the most important leader in the business life of New York during his generation.

Moses Taylor had invested heavily in the stock of the Lackawanna Railroad. In point of fact, at one time he owned nearly all of it. So, in 1864, Samuel Sloan was elected to the Board of Managers and in 1867 became president of the Lackawanna. He was to remain in office thirty-two years.

Numerous expansion plans of the Delaware, Lackawanna and Western had been held up by the Civil War, including an extension of the line from Pennsylvania down through New Jersey to Philadelphia or New York. When Sloan became president, the situation was much as it had been seven years before. The board was neatly divided on the subject of what direction developments ought to take. One group of directors, listening to S. B. Chittenden, favored a consolidation with the Central Railroad of New Jersey. Another faction, approved by Sloan, was in favor of leasing the Morris and Essex Railroad, which had physical contact with the Lackawanna at Delaware Water Gap.

Sloan discovered that General John Brisbin, superintendent of the Delaware, Lackawanna and Western, and president of the road between 1863 and 1867, was the real leader of the opposition. He encouraged John I. Blair and John J. Phelps to increase their holdings in Morris and Essex stock and conducted a quiet personal campaign to win over one or two directors who opposed him. At the annual meeting in 1868 Sloan polled a substantial vote. Brisbin and other managers later retired.

The warmth and easy accessibility of his Hudson River days seem to have been pretty well rubbed off Samuel Sloan when he began to pick up the loose ends of the postwar Lackawanna. Few of the old-timers recall that he was even affable. Perhaps he had no reason to be.

His field officer in operations was William Hallstead, who left his impress on a whole generation of railroad men. The word had gone out of the president's office that the trains were going to run on time, that contracts with shippers of freight or buyers of coal were going to be kept to the letter, that rolling stock and roadbed were to be kept in repair. And Hallstead, superintendent of the whole line north of Delaware Water Gap, announced that he was going to make a personal issue out of enforcing the order.

For years the most familiar sight at the Scranton station was Bill Hallstead on the platform with his watch in his hand, checking the time of train arrivals. He had little cause for complaint. In his way he was a martinet. He was gruff and tough and uncompromising. But he was not unjust. He would listen to an argument, and he had the respect of the workers. During his time the Lackawanna had fewer delays and fewer accidents than ever before in its history and came to be reputed the best-run railroad in the United States.

As the carriers improved and extended, competition increased, there were rate wars, rebates to shippers, business tactics which in some parts of the country were only a little short of prohibition mob techniques.

The rate agreement adopted by the coal carriers in 1870, under Sloan's arbitration, was broken in 1876, and immediately all the anthracite roads were in trouble. Lackawanna stock dropped from over 100 to 64. New Jersey Central was taken over by a receiver. Reading delayed the inevitable by making a deal with its creditors but eventually went into a receivership also. In 1875 Lackawanna was still slipping.

Cutthroat competition reached a point at which virtually every railroad was on its own, with every other railroad against it. Hostile legislation by the states presently brought on the Interstate Commerce Commission.

As usual Sloan had great foresight. It was plain to him that the government was presently going to object to a relationship on a basis of interlocking directorates between the railroads and the producing companies whose products they carried. The only salvation of the anthracite roads, as he saw it, was for them to free themselves from limitations. He advocated, and got, extensions north and west, and finally, by running a line into Buffalo, made the Lackawanna an important factor in the handling of general freight.

To make freight cars interchangeable in this scheme, it became necessary for the Lackawanna to abandon the old gauge of 6 feet and shift to the standard gauge of 4 feet 8½ inches in use east and west of Buffalo.

The Lackawanna, fortunately, had no such difficulties as the riots conducted by the pie salesmen and hot-sausage merchants at Erie, Pennsylvania, where the adoption of a single gauge made it unnecessary for passengers to change cars. But there was enough grief for any man. The change was made in 1876, at which time the rehabilitation of the road had been pretty well completed. Hundreds of freight cars and passenger coaches had to be equipped with new axles, and scores of locomotives had to be made over.

The total cost of alterations to rolling stock and track cost something over a million and a quarter dollars. But the cost was not what bothered Sloan and Hallstead. It was the job of getting an army of track workers to perform this one job with the split-second timing of a ballet. And it was done just that way.

For months construction crews had been at work laying a continuous third rail 1 foot 3½ inches inside the right-hand rail of the old track as they proceeded north. On a Sunday, crews with prefabricated switches were at every station and siding on the road to complete the hiatuses in the new line. And in twenty-four hours trains were running again. Every single haul was on time to the second that day. If it had not been, Bill Hallstead would have taken somebody's scalp with his bare hands.

The results of the changes were evident almost immediately. Lackawanna which had been selling at 30 went to 94. Sloan lived to see his great anthracite carrier, cleaned up and comfortable, getting a reputation as a fast passenger route. While coal shipments between 1881 and 1890 were up 32 per cent, general freight traffic had increased 160 per cent and passenger business 85 per cent. In 1885 stock sold at 129. Dividends of 7 per cent were paid regularly from 1885 to 1904.

If results mean anything, Samuel Sloan had learned how to be a good railroad executive, and he got plenty of practice. He was elected president of the Michigan Central Railroad in June, 1876 and served for two years. For several years he was also president of the Père Marquette Railroad of Michigan; Fort Wayne and Jackson Railroad of Indiana; Rome, Watertown and Ogdensburg Railroad of New York; and the International and Great Northern Railroad of Texas.

He resigned the presidency of the Lackawanna in 1899 and remained on the Board of Managers as chairman for the remaining eight years of his life. He was ninety years old when he died in 1907 and had been running railroads for more than fifty years. Railroads had not been in existence much longer than that.

16 *New Railroad*

WHEN William H. Truesdale took over the presidency of the Delaware, Lackawanna and Western Railroad in 1899, he found what was still primarily a coal road, although also a well-formed passenger route. Sloan had seen the need for a more diversified service and had started a change-over in policy that was already showing results. Still, in 1900, Truesdale's first full year, 40 per cent of the company's revenues was derived from the transportation of coal; 30 per cent, other freight; and 20 per cent, passengers. The completeness of the change during the Truesdale regime may be seen in the comparison of these figures with the percentages of 1924, in which coal represents only about 27 per cent of the operating revenues; other freight, 45 per cent; and passengers, 15 per cent. And this in spite of the fact that the total volume of coal, in actual tons, handled by the road in 1924 was twice as large as the tonnage in 1900.

If anybody said that Truesdale had made the road over, he would probably be right.

No one man can be said to have produced the miracle of the Lackawanna out of a few miles of strap rail and a pile of coal. But there are periods during its hundred years when the metamorphosis has been more noticeable, and one of these, undoubtedly, was during the Truesdale administration. Without neglecting its coal traffic, which continued to be an important and dependable source of income, the new president had built up the road to meet competition for other classes of traffic. The cost had been staggering and almost unceasing over a period of twenty-six years. But long before the end of the modernization program the road had a physical plant that railroad experts were coming from all over the world to see. The one-time coal carrier was famous as The Line of Phoebe Snow and could advertise itself with considerable truth as "mile for mile the most highly developed railroad in America."

Mr. Truesdale was the first Lackawanna president who had not been an importer or banker or engaged in some other business before coming into the transportation business. In 1899 he had held a railroad job of one variety or another for thirty years, with a thorough grounding in the handling of freight.

He was born on December 1, 1851, near Youngstown, Ohio, and got his education in the public schools of Rock Island, Illinois. When he was eighteen years old, he got a job with the Rockford, Rock Island and St. Louis Railroad (now part of the Burlington system) as a clerk in the auditing department. Later he served as cashier and, still later, as purchasing agent for the same road.

In 1872 and 1873 he was transfer agent for the company in Frankfort, Germany. In 1875 he went into the office of Osborn and Curtis, railroad attorneys in Rock Island, to get some knowledge of the fundamentals of railroad law. A year later he was appointed assistant to the receiver and treasurer of the Logansport, Crawfordsville and Southwestern Railroad (now a part of the Pennsylvania) at Terre Haute, Indiana. Three years afterward he became general freight agent for the same road.

In 1881 he was appointed assistant traffic manager of the Chicago, St. Paul, Minneapolis and Omaha Railroad. He became assistant to the president of the Minneapolis and St. Louis in January, 1883, and was elected vice-president in May of the same year. He was advanced to the presidency in 1887 and in the following year was appointed receiver. He was then thirty-seven years old.

Truesdale went to the Chicago, Rock Island and Pacific Railroad in 1894 as third vice-president and advanced through the grades— second vice-president and general manager in 1897; first vice-president and general manager in 1898. On March 1, 1899, he was elected president of the Delaware, Lackawanna and Western Railroad, with headquarters in New York.

In 1900 the company's balance sheet showed a cost of road and equipment of about $25,000,000. In 1924 this figure had risen to approximately $96,000,000. In 1900 the cost of equipment was about half the investment in road. In 1924 these two items were very nearly equal. All of which epitomizes Truesdale's simple but expensive policy. If you want to carry freight, you have to have the equipment to carry it and a road to roll it on.

The Lackawanna was one of the first railroads in the United States to equip all of its main-line mileage with automatic block signals, with the result that it has had very few bad accidents.

From the beginning of the Truesdale administration the road consistently added to its mileage of third and fourth main tracks, permitting the uninterrupted movement of passengers and high-grade merchandise. In the same period the Lackawanna began to justify a boast that its suburban service was the best in the New York area. When he retired in 1925 to take the chairmanship of the Lackawanna Board of Managers, Truesdale turned over one of the most modern railroads in America.

Among the chief difficulties confronting William H. Truesdale when he became president of the Lackawanna were a long and difficult passage over the Dansville hills, another one over the Alleghenies, a Chinese puzzle on top of the Poconos and a 40-mile time waster in New Jersey. He had the shortest road between Hoboken and Buffalo, but he also had the slowest curves and the steepest grades.

Probably the most striking feature of the Lackawanna's line between Summit, New Jersey, and Buffalo is its splendid detachment from everything else. It rides amazingly for some three hundred miles on the rooftree of the world, following the tops of mountain ridges and leaping across wide valleys cloudily alone.

The mathematicians tell you that all this is just a matter of maintenance of grade. But your eyes tell you that, to maintain the grade so that trains may travel at a speed of as much as 80 miles an hour in most parts of the route over the Alleghenies, men of imagination have built one of the country's outstanding engineering marvels.

In the beginning—a few years after the Reverend John Miller had made the journey from Providence to Clark's Summit with a team and a 400-pound load in something like fourteen hours—the course of the Ligett's Gap Railroad to Great Bend was slow and none too certain. Its designers had learned something of grades from their construction of gravity railroads in the vicinity. In fact, the organizers of the road had listened interestedly to the proposal of James Archbald that the entire route be laid out in a series of inclined planes with stationary steam engines to furnish the power. But the rocky gorges of the Alleghenies did not lend themselves readily to theory. The first miracle of the Ligett's Gap road was that it was able to cling to the mountainside on its climb out of Scranton through the Gap. The second was that an engine could follow its course from there to the Susquehanna River.

"Old Puff," the locomotive affectionately described in early reminiscence of the Lackawanna, was not much different from other motive power of the times. These engines ran fairly well on the flat, unless the track happened to get wet. They could climb easy grades if the firemen stoked them to a high pressure, if they were not pulling too much weight, and if they did not blow up. Looking at the old right-of-way today, you realize that such lines as this were the proof that steam had come to stay. If a tin teapot could make the run from Scranton to Great Bend on a wet day, it could go anywhere.

It is interesting to think that, had Scranton been situated so that a railroad could be built on a flat surface to a market, the amazing lines over the mountains might have been a long time coming. Elsewhere the pioneer roads were being constructed along lines handed down by the canal builders, through wide valleys or along lake beaches. But not in Scranton's neighborhood. There the coal producers had been forced to haul their output up and down steep declivities, and their first railways had been only a step or two removed from the modern elevator. Fortunately, by experience they got some knowledge of how steep a slope an engine would climb. Lacking such empirical knowledge, nobody in his right mind would ever have attempted to put a line from Scranton up through "The Notch."

Once "Old Puff" was puffing over this hump, the amateur engineers seem to have quit babying it. The rest of the route for the next sixty years was virtually in the tracks of the ox teams that had hauled the Scranton rails to the Erie in 1848.

There were some beastly hills in this forty-odd miles. There was a steep descent for the crossing of Tunkhannock Creek and a climb at Hop Bottom. About the only level spots in the route were in front of the stations.

In the beginning, to cross the valleys, the road was set up on wooden trestles, gradually filled in with earth, as previously explained. One airy stretch of logwork carried the line over Tunkhannock Mountain pending the completion of the Tunkhannock Tunnel. And even after the opening of the tunnel, this particular ridge remained one of the country's major railroad hazards.

The gauge of the road, conforming to that of the Erie, was 6 feet. The engines, on the lines of the "Spitfire," London-built for the Reading Railroad and bought by the Ligett's Gap line after having run 189,268 miles, burned wood and were reasonably sturdy. Despite haphazard grades, such engines as this quickly earned their keep. E. J. Rauch, an early engineer, reported that he had hauled forty-five four-wheeled cars with the "Spitfire," each containing 4½ tons of freight.

Rauch, who lived to a ripe old age despite his service on experimental railroads in the Alleghenies, left an illuminating account of his routine, which was printed by *Railway Age* in 1900. The chief feature of it was his story of a typical run.

He described an unpleasant night at Great Bend in the fall of 1853, as he waited with the Lackawanna mail train for the Erie passenger train from New York. The Erie was already four hours late and would be later. But no matter. The Lackawanna mail connection must wait.

The rain showed little sign of letting up. The platform was running water in rivers, and, more seriously, the tracks were awash. He had some protection in the cab of his engine, for which he was truly grateful. There had been a time, not so long before, when the engine crew performed their wonders out in the open. Some superintendents objected to the addition of the cab, on the ground that engineers and firemen would be getting soft.

The tender behind the locomotive was stacked high with green wood cut up into three-foot billets. It had two brake wheels, one on each side, for separate control of front and rear trucks. The wood was wet and getting wetter, and the fireman was taking a very sour view of it.

The engine, somewhat muddied up, displayed a lot of polished brass and a name, "Lightning." In proportion to the small boiler, the drive wheels and stack seemed huge. The 6-foot gauge made the whole machine seem flat and ungainly. Inside the cab were few of the controls required for the running of a modern locomotive. There were three or four gauge cocks, a throttle lever, reversing lever, a rope for the bell, and another for the whistle. There was no injector and, in the absence of a stack with an arresting device, the sparks would flow back onto the train in a continuous shower.

The headlight of the Erie train presently appeared in the distance, a hazy spot of brightness in the rain. And in no time at all, the New York express came rattling up to the platform. There was no surprise. Everybody knew that the headlight could not have been seen more than a couple of hundred yards away.

Passengers and mails were quickly transferred to the Lackawanna coaches, women in bulky crinolines that made three a crowd in any coach, men in fur caps and homespuns or in tall beaver hats, frock coats, and tight trousers, as befitted the dignity of travel in the trains. The chief personal luggage was carpetbags. The conductor, thinking of a dry bed in Scranton, swore vigorously at a roustabout who had momentarily mislaid the Scranton mail, such as it was. He did not emphasize his haste by looking at his watch. He had no watch.

In due time he gave a starting signal, and the Ligett's Gap train slowly pulled out onto the wooden bridge spanning the Susquehanna. The river was bankfull and turbulent. Mr. Rauch, the brave engineer up in the cab, took a look at it and knew what to expect from the creeks up ahead.

Once off the bridge, the engine, laboring against a strong quartering wind and gasping asthmatically because of a defective valve cutoff, started up the slope to New Milford Summit. Rauch, wet to the skin and already numb with cold, was nevertheless leaning out of his cab window into the rain trying to see a few feet into the blackness. Now and again he reached a hand to try the gauge cocks and lifted a practiced ear to find out whether they were blowing steam or water. He could not see the landmarks of the route or anything much except the plume of sparks falling away to the rear of the stack. In the words of a later breed of pilots, he was driving by the seat of his pants.

The fireman, stooping forward with legs wide apart, was almost ceaselessly jamming sticks of wood into the firebox, filling every corner from the fire ring to the lower row of flues. From the open door a diverging column of light shot high into the night, like the tail of a comet, giving the passengers a disconcerting view of lurching engine and bouncing tender as the little tin teapot hit the dangerously soft places in the track.

Over the summit the train, encouraged by the engineer, gathered a rattling speed of perhaps thirty miles an hour. It would have to be slowed down pretty soon for Tunkhannock Mountain. The tunnel, after nearly five years of work, was not finished yet, and there would be a lot of time lost in the zigzag, switchback climb over tunnel hill. In the meantime Rauch was trying to gain what minutes he could on a fairly straight stretch of downgrade.

Then, suddenly, there was a light ahead—right in the middle of the track.

It was not moving. The engineer could hardly see it in the rain. It did not seem to be a signal. No signal would be as small as that, Rauch told himself, and it certainly would not be so still.

But the engineer's reflexes worked automatically, even if his conscious mind did not. While he was still arguing with himself, he slammed the throttle lever shut, sounded the whistle, went into reverse, and poured on the sand. Without being told, the fireman was bearing down on the brake wheels.

All of these things happened in a matter of seconds, and presently the train had slowed to a crawl. As it drew near the light, still perfectly stationary and straight ahead, the engineer made out the figure of a man between the rails, bareheaded and waving his hat. As the engine stopped a few feet from him, he bent to pick up a lantern, a tallow dip with a glass cover. He was obviously a farmer. His hair, beard, and clothes were streaming with rain.

"What's the matter?" roared the engineer.

"Wal," drawled the apparition, "mebbe you better git down and see. Looks like as if this bridge ain't too safe."

Rauch swung off the engine and followed the farmer's bobbing lantern down the track. Presently he stopped and the engineer peered over his shoulder.

"Bridge!" gasped Rauch. "Man alive! There ain't no bridge!"

"Just what I was a-thinkin'," agreed the farmer. "It's down the creek a piece."

And then all at once train crew and passengers were crowding about in the rain, trying to wring the farmer's hand and making hysterical speeches. Rauch belatedly thought of a question that had been puzzling him since he first got down from the cab.

"Look," he said, "I almost didn't stop because I couldn't make out your signal. Why didn't you wave your lantern?"

"Because," answered the farmer lucidly, "I was a-wavin' of my hat."

In the life of every railroad there is somebody with a lantern who crawls out into the tempest to halt the train before it hits the hole where the bridge used to be. But few of these heroes ever made so casual an affair of it as the hat-waving farmer at Oakley's trestle. Nobody bothered to take his name. Apparently he went home— wherever that was—and no railroad man ever saw him again. He lives in Lackawanna legend, not so much for saving the train as for his eccentricity in signaling.

The Tunkhannock Tunnel was opened presently—about the time Superintendent Dotterer solved the problem of burning anthracite in engines. After that the passage to Big Bend was less of an adventure, although for years it retained most of the surprises of a roller coaster.

In the other direction from Scranton, the Delaware and Cobb's Gap line wandered up Roaring Brook to the top of the Poconos over another one of James Archbald's surveys. It twisted no end, and it skipped between loftier peaks than the Ligett's Gap road and came down to Stroudsburg and Delaware Water Gap in one long dive.

The assembly of these two lines, amplified by another mountain climb through the western edge of the Finger Lakes district and by some pretty rugged New Jersey uplifts in the Morris and Essex leasehold, was looked upon by some as the longest hurdle race in American railroad practice. No fireman who ever had to shovel coal on any division of it between Hoboken and Buffalo will argue with the indictment.

From the Delaware Water Gap the route followed the Warren Railroad line into New Jersey, through Delaware, Manunka Chunk, and Warren to Washington, then northeast over the Morris and Essex to Lake Hopatcong. This course through a generally rugged district was strictly along the lines of least resistance. Apparently tired out after its long dash through the clouds, the railroad climbed no hills that it did not have to. But it was not so particular about curves. It wandered along a circuitous path nearly 40 miles long, with fifty-seven curves over which a train covered six full circles. Despite its preference for valleys, the road had a rise and fall of 248 feet.

All except the stretch between Binghamton and Buffalo—which was the newest and the least of Truesdale's worries—had been in operation nearly fifty years when he inherited them, and during a half century they had not changed perceptibly. There had been numerous changes in alignment and grade, of course, and, presumably, it had been made somewhat easier to get trains from Hoboken into northern New York. But it was obvious that the sort of modernization that would do any good must be something like building a new railroad.

In 1908 he was given authority to do just that.

17 *Man-made Mountains*

In a modernization program as extensive as that inaugurated by Mr. Truesdale much responsibility devolves upon the chief engineer, and the Lackawanna has been most fortunate in the men chosen to fill that very important post. When Mr. Truesdale took over the management he brought to the property as chief engineer Mr. W. K. McFarlin, who established his reputation on Western railroads. He served the Lackawanna in that capacity with distinction until 1903. At that time he resigned to enter private contracting business. He was succeeded by Mr. Lincoln Bush, who came from the Chicago and North Western Railroad Company to serve under Mr. McFarlin as bridge engineer. Mr. Bush served as chief engineer from 1903 until December 31, 1908.

As chief engineer, Mr. Bush built at the Lackawanna's Hoboken Terminal the first low umbrella type of train shed ever built, with direct openings over the tracks to carry off smoke and steam from locomotives. This shed became known as the Bush Train Shed, and the type has been extensively used. Mr. Bush also made the first use of the sand jack for lowering heavy bridges in connection with rebuilding of the heavy drawbridges over the Hackensack and Passaic rivers.

It was while Mr. Bush was still chief engineer that the change of alignment known as the Hopatcong-Slateford cutoff was located and the plans developed, including the concrete bridges built on that line.

On January 1, 1909, George J. Ray was appointed chief engineer to succeed Mr. Bush.

Ray was born in Metamora, Illinois, on March 24, 1876, got an A.B. degree at the University of Illinois in 1898, a civil engineering degree in 1910, and a D.Sc. from Lafayette College, Easton, Pennsylvania, in 1916. He was rodman, transitman, assistant engineer, track supervisor, and roadmaster for the Illinois Central Railroad between 1898 and 1903. With the Lackawanna he was division engineer from 1903 to 1909, chief engineer from 1909 to 1919. He served for a year as engineering assistant to the Eastern Division, U.S. Railroad Administration, and returned to the Lackawanna as chief engineer in 1920. He was vice-president and general manager of the road from 1934 until his retirement in 1946.

Ray is a man with a quick, adaptable mind, whose chief asset is an all-embracing and retentive memory. In the first few months of his service with the Lackawanna he had been up and down the line repeatedly. He studied every curve and grade and cut and fill until he had a detailed picture of the road filed away in his mind. And when he was called upon to discuss the problems of improvement, he knew what he was talking about.

As chief engineer Ray had charge of the construction work, including the bridges, on the Hopatcong-Slateford cutoff. He was given an opportunity the like of which falls into the hands of one engineer in a million. And he made the most of it.

His theory of construction, as exemplified in the Hopatcong-Slateford cutoff, was considered revolutionary when he outlined it, but the Board of Managers of the Lackawanna had grown weary of trying to get along with standardized makeshifts. Instead of following rivers on their leisurely courses, he proposed to cut across the drainage of the country at right angles, to lop off the tops of some mountains and use the earth and rock to make others, to lay out a line without grades or curves. And he virtually did it. The new line has a total length of 28 miles as against the 40 miles of the old one. The grade does not exceed one half of one per cent. The total rise and fall is 11 feet and the fifteen curves add up to one complete circle. The project cost $11,000,000.

The Lackawanna of New Jersey, which was given a special charter for the construction, started work in the summer of 1908 and opened the line to traffic in the winter of 1911. Considerable progress had been made in railroad construction since the first raw crews had begun to hang a line to the mountainside at Clark's Summit fifty years before. But earth removal was still a matter of men with shovels and horses with scoops. It is difficult, looking at the work now, to figure how any amount of manpower could have got it done in three and a half years.

During the peak of construction, networks of narrow-gauge line were branching out from the main right-of-way like the veins of a leaf. Fifty narrow-gauge engines puffed up and down these wandering byways, hauling trains of dump trucks. Standard-gauge work trains were pushed forward as rapidly as feasible. And supplying these carriers were twenty of the largest steam shovels then available. The shovels, edging up on the heels of blasting crews, pried the rock out of the hills. The dump-car trains rolled it on into the valleys. Simultaneously forms were erected for two of the world's largest railroad bridges, and in the entire line seventy-three bridges, culverts, and viaducts of reinforced concrete were poured, while railroad builders from all parts of the world came to watch. Until that time reinforced concrete was a material that railroad construction engineers did not much care for.

Ray listened politely to the objections of his visitors. But he did not worry about them. He had put the concrete through rigorous tests, and he knew what it would do. Besides, it was a flexible material and quickly worked.

A trainload of dynamite was required to crack open the rocky hills. The total excavation, if it had gone into ditch digging, would have made a canal 16 feet wide, 8 feet deep, and 550 miles long. All the material produced by this digging was promptly swallowed up by the tremendous fills, and still there was not enough. To maintain the level of these man-made plateaus across broad, gentle valleys, the shovels had to produce an additional tonnage of earth equivalent to a one-foot cut over an area of 12 square miles. Enough steel went into the concrete work to build a railroad 15 miles long and enough concrete to pave 40 miles of modern express highway.

The principal difference between the Hopatcong-Slateford line and other cutoffs lies in its grandiose conception. Like all such routes, it is a series of alternate cuts and fills. The cuts are wide slices through slate and shale and granite, some of them deep enough to hide a ten-story building. The fills rise from the valleys to a corresponding height. One of them, over Pequest Valley, is the world's largest railroad embankment, over three miles long with a maximum height of 110 feet. This is truly high iron, and the view from it is a breathtaking panorama. Far below and to the north lies the village of Andover, site of early American iron furnaces. From this weird observation point, it looks like something in another world.

Beyond Johnsonburg Station, as one moves west, the road passes through the Armstrong Cut, the largest on the cutoff. It is a mile long and has a maximum depth of 104 feet. Eight hundred fifty thousand cubic yards of material came out of this slot, enough to load 21,000 average-sized gondolas, a train about two hundred miles long.

The two concrete bridges at the west end of the cutoff were once objects of awed attention from engineers and amateur photographers and would be still, were it not for more impressive structures of the same sort on the line from Scranton to Binghamton. Paulins Kill Viaduct near Blairstown—the only station open to passenger traffic on the cutoff—is 1,100 feet long and 117 feet above the valley, which it spans on seven arches.

After another high fill and a deep cut on a curve, the road comes into the Delaware Valley and crosses the river, a state highway, and the old Lackawanna line on another concrete viaduct. This one, 64 feet above water level, is carried by nine arches for a distance of 1,140 feet. At the west end of the bridge the road curves sharply north and merges with the old line at Slateford Junction.

And then there was the "improvement" between Scranton and the Susquehanna River. They built an entirely new railroad there and, in a grandiose gesture, gave the old one to their competitors, the truckers, in the form of a state highway.

There are few stretches of railroad in the world so startling as this—none more so. The line climbs, as it always did, from Scranton to Clark's Summit, but now, having achieved the top, it stays there, virtually at a level, on one of the highest ridges in the Alleghenies till it makes a leisurely descent into the valley of the Susquehanna at Hallstead (named after Bill, the great timekeeper). The sheer audacity of its concept makes it one of the most remarkable exhibits in that part of Pennsylvania.

Mountain lands fall away from it on either side, rocky gorges and the slanting planes of cultivation and forests and rivers stretching away into misty distances. It is always beautiful, with a covering of greenery and wild flowers in the spring, or snow in winter, and it unfolds in one continuous panorama. But the most memorable thing about it is a part of the railroad itself, the Tunkhannock Viaduct, which Theodore Dreiser called "a new wonder of the world."

Starting from Scranton, you come onto it through the Factory-ville Tunnel, which is in one spot where the engineers did not care to go over the top. And you need only one glimpse of it to know that there is nothing like it in America.

It is not merely the largest concrete railroad bridge ever built, but one of the most graceful structures in the world. For sheer, simple beauty, it is not likely to be matched in a year's travel.

For centuries people have been journeying to Nîmes in southern France to look at the Pont du Gard, put up nineteen centuries ago by the Romans. It is one of the finest examples of Roman masonry —smooth stones laid without cement—and probably it will never be duplicated in this world. But most people who travel thousands of miles to look on it have little interest in it as a fine mechanical job. They remember it as an example of awesome beauty combined with almost overpowering size. It fills the eye as it fills the Gard Valley. Sightseers stop a quarter of a mile away, gaze up at it, and speak in whispers.

Tunkhannock Viaduct is instantly reminiscent of the old Roman bridge. Pont du Gard gets its altitude through three tiers of arches of diminishing size. Tunkhannock has two rows, but the effect is the same. Tunkhannock has the same vaulting grace, the same moving quality, and gives the same impression of being afloat in the air. The only thing it lacks, you would surmise, is the *size* that made the Pont du Gard unique.

And then you look at the figures:

Pont du Gard is 870 feet long; Tunkhannock Viaduct is very nearly three times that. Pont du Gard is 160 feet high; Tunkhannock, 240 feet. Martin's Creek Viaduct, a similar structure nine miles further on the road to Binghamton, is 1,600 feet long and very nearly the same height as the Pont du Gard. But nobody pays any attention

to it. The Tunkhannock Viaduct contains 167,000 cubic yards of
concrete and more than a thousand tons of reinforcing steel. Its
height above bedrock, on which it is based, is in places 338 feet.

Despite the fact that the Tunkhannock Viaduct has no world-
wide fame, it cannot be said to be neglected. People in the neighborhood drive out to look at it and take their friends to see it, as a
matter of course. Occasionally a passenger gets off a train in Scranton
or Binghamton and rides a local back to Nicholson to make sure
that his eyes have not deceived him. The automobile road that
follows the old railroad right-of-way is naturally one of easy grades
and wide curves. It is paved now and makes this marvel easy of
access for anybody 50 miles east or west.

Over this road in 1916 came Theodore Dreiser on his "Hoosier
holiday," thoroughly dissatisfied with much that he saw, annoyed
by trains that carried coal, and in a thoroughly bad temper. And
then, all at once, he got a surprise.

He wrote: *

North of Factoryville a little way—perhaps a score of miles,—we en-
countered one of those amazing works of man which, if they become
numerous enough, eventually make a country a great memory. . . .
They are the bones of the body politic which, like the roads and viaducts and paths of ancient Rome, testify to the prime of its physical
strength. . . .

We were coming around a curve near Nicholson, Pennsylvania, approaching a stream which traverses this great valley, when across it from
ridge's edge to ridge's edge suddenly appeared a great white stone or
concrete viaduct or bridge—we could not tell at once, which—a thing
so colossal and impressive that we instantly stopped the car so that we
might remain and gaze at it. Ten huge arches—each say two hundred
feet wide and two hundred feet high—were (each) topped by eleven
other arches, say fifteen feet wide and forty feet high, and this whole
surmounted by a great roadbed carrying several railway tracks—we
assumed. The builders were still at work on it.

As before the great cathedral at Rheims or Amiens or Canterbury, or
those giant baths in Rome which so gratify the imagination, so here at
Nicholson, in a valley celebrated for nothing in particular and at the
edge of a town of no size, we stood before this vast structure, gazing
in a sort of awe.

* DREISER, THEODORE, *Hoosier Holiday*, Simon and Schuster, New York.

Those arches! How really beautiful they were! How wide, how high, how noble, how symmetrically planned! And the smaller arches above, how delicate and lightsomely graceful! How could they carry a heavy train so high in the air? But there they were, two hundred and fifty feet above us from the stream's surface, so we discovered afterwards, and the whole structure nearly twenty-four hundred feet long.

We learned that it was the work of a great railroad corporation—part of a scheme for shortening its line about three miles!—which, incidentally was leaving a monument to the American of this day which would be stared at for centuries to come as evidencing the courage, the resourcefulness, the taste, the wealth, the commerce and the force of the time which we are living—now.

It is rather odd to stand in the presence of so great a thing in the making and realize that you are looking at one of the true wonders of the world. . . .

Nicholson is a typical American country community, which derives its living from the small but fertile farms that lie hidden away in folds of the Tunkhannock Valley. It tends its cattle and reaps its grain and sends its children to typical schools and is interested mostly in rain and crops and markets. But it is not the same as other farm towns in northern Pennsylvania. It is dominated by the viaduct.

Here, in front of the drugstore, you are suddenly aware of the utter magnificence of the imagination that drew that great white streak across the sky. No matter where you look, unless you turn your back upon it, you are aware of its lacy arches, its beauty, and its towering strength. And you realize that only a blind man could live in its shadow without being constantly moved by it.

Like Dreiser, we came to Nicholson one day by car, not entirely unprepared, for we had frequently made the attempt to take in the full sweep of the great bridge from the upper air. The driver, as he told us on the way from Scranton, was no stranger to the place, either. He seemed to be a typical taxi driver, wise and practical and brittle. He had had a high-school education, a hitch in the mines, and had been graduated from the Marines by a bullet on one of the Jap islands. He was married and deeply concerned with the problems of raising a family in a new and strange world. But as we alighted at the foot of Main Street to look up at the bridge, so did he. And his comment was surely the equal of any of Dreiser's.

"My God!" he said. "What poets they ought to be able to raise in this place!"

The Clark's Summit–Hallstead cutoff is only 39⁹⁄₁₀ miles long, although it seems longer as you twist and roll along the old road's line of abandoned stations. They are lunchrooms, now, or harness shops or hardware stores or feed warehouses, from forty to a couple of hundred feet below the high iron of the new right-of-way.

Figures show that the new route is only about three miles shorter than the old one. And you may remember some of the argument in the technical journals over where the profit could lie in spending $12,000,000 to save three miles. But as you stand and watch a long train streaking at a mile a minute across the sky you begin to get some idea of what a saving of 3.6 miles meant. Eleven full circles of curves were cut down to four, and hundreds of feet of rise and fall were eliminated. President Truesdale, commenting on the work in November, 1915, pointed out that the saving in operating cost alone would have made it worth while.

"There are other things besides the shortening of distance to be considered," he said. "The new road will give us a maximum grade of .68 per cent, as against a previous maximum of 1.23 per cent, and a greatly reduced curvature. These, to the layman, may seem like small and unimportant results. But, together, the changes will cut the running time of every passenger train between New York and Buffalo by twenty minutes, and in the case of freights will reduce running time a full half hour. Nor is this all; through reduction of grade, they will make it possible to move trains with two engines which, under present conditions, require five."

He was speaking, of course, of conditions as they existed in 1916, but they still obtain.

The modernizing of the main line brought about some changes in the Pocono Mountains. Some curves were straightened; some grades flattened; the long roll from Cresco to Stroudsburg was made more gentle. But in the main, the stretch of track between Scranton and Delaware Water Gap follows the same course as the original Cobb's Gap Railroad.

18 *The Coal Business*

DURING William H. Truesdale's administration the Lackawanna made vast changes in its corporate structure. By 1906 the railroad was well on its way to being a freight and passenger carrier of national importance, but it was still pretty well identified with its dusty origins. It was still one of the great anthracite roads, deriving much of its income from the business of mining, buying, transporting, and selling coal. Which means that it was squarely in the province of the Commodities Clause of the Hepburn Act.

This clause, which became part of a Federal law in 1906, provided that after May 1, 1908, it would be unlawful for any railroad to transport in interstate commerce any commodity, other than timber, manufactured, "mined or produced by it, or under its authority, or which it may own in whole or in part, or in which it may have any interest, except such as may be necessary . . . for its use in the conduct of its business as a common carrier." The purpose of the law was, in general, to prevent railroads from acting as public carriers and private shippers at the same time. Its immediate effect was to disrupt the operating methods of the Lackawanna.

First, to stay within the law, the railroad had to get rid of all interest in the coal it carried, and the most simple answer to the problem seemed to be to sell it at the breakers in Pennsylvania before it should have to be transported anywhere at all. To that end The Delaware, Lackawanna and Western Coal Company was incorporated under the laws of New Jersey to supersede the coal sales department of the railroad. The capital stock of the new company was fixed at $6,800,000 with shares at $50 each.

Railroad stockholders were invited to subscribe to the stock of the coal company at a rate of one share for each four shares of railroad stock. Ninety-nine per cent of the Lackawanna stockholders did subscribe, paying for their stock in part out of a 50 per cent cash dividend previously declared.

E. E. Loomis, vice-president of the Lackawanna Railroad in charge of coal operations, was elected president of the coal company, and other officers and directors of the railroad were given posts on the new board. The railroad company and the coal company then drew up a contract whereby the following provisions were accepted: (1) The railroad would sell to the coal company all coal mined or acquired at a price, on prepared sizes, of 65 per cent of the New York price on the day of delivery. (2) The amount of coal sold would be at the option of the railroad company, and the coal company agreed not to buy any coal from any other source. (3) The coal company would conduct its sales to the best interests of the railroad. (4) The railroad company would lease to the coal company all its trestles, docks, and shipping facilities. The contract was signed by representatives of both companies on August 2, 1909.

Outwardly, thereafter, the Lackawanna's coal business went on much as before. The railroad mined about 7,000,000 tons a year and bought about 1,500,000 tons from mines along its lines. Holding back 1,500,000 tons for use in its own operations, it sold 7,000,000 tons to the coal company at the breakers, and it hauled just about the same amount of coal away from the Scranton district to markets in New York or elsewhere. The difference was—from a cursory point of view—that the railroad was now carrying the coal company's coal and not its own.

In February, 1913, the government filed a petition against both corporations, alleging that they were virtually identical and that the railroad retained too much of an interest in the coal to carry it legally in interstate commerce. The suit was tried in the U.S. District Court for the District of New Jersey and a decision returned in favor of the defendants. The railroad company did not own the coal, the court declared, the two corporations were not identical, and the railroad corporation had acted in good faith in its attempt to comply with the provisions of the Hepburn Act.

The government, however, took an appeal to the U.S. Supreme Court, which, on June 21, 1915, reversed the decision of the lower court and enjoined the railroad company from transporting coal under the terms of its contract with the coal company. The Supreme Court found that the railroad company had retained a sufficient interest in the coal to make its transportation unlawful under the statute.

The Lackawanna railroad company, apparently not too much surprised by the ruling of the high court, drew up new contracts with the coal company and rearranged its corporate structure. The coal company elected new officers who did not hold similar positions in the railroad corporation. Restrictive provisions were left out of the new contract, and the price arrangement for the sale of coal at 65 per cent of the price at tidewater was abandoned.

This arrangement was thoroughly legal and in accordance with the Supreme Court's interpretation of the prohibitions of the Commodities Clause. The railroad was thus able to keep its coal properties and go on with its business of mining. And so things went until 1921, when the Board of Managers of the Lackawanna wanted to issue more capital stock and, as representatives of a Pennsylvania corporation, found themselves bound by the General Act of the Pennsylvania Legislature of 1901 authorizing such increases.

The original charter of the railroad authorized an increase in capital stock solely for the construction of its owned lines in Pennsylvania, and the proposed issue was for a general improvement program embracing three states. The necessary authority had to be found elsewhere—and was, under the General Act of 1901.

This act provided that such a corporation as the Lackawanna might, with full consent of the stockholders, increase capital stock to the extent necessary to carry on and enlarge its business. But there was a catch in the provision. It was stated that the act would not relieve from prior limitations any railroad that had not accepted all the provisions of Article XVII of the Pennsylvania Constitution.

The Pennsylvania Constitution had been adopted in 1874, many years subsequent to the passage of the special acts that together constituted the Lackawanna's charter. Section Ten of Article XVII of the Constitution provided that no railroad in existence at the time of its adoption should have the benefit of any General Laws subsequently enacted, unless the railroad agreed to accept all the provisions of Article XVII. The part of Article XVII relating to the railroads had prohibited them from mining or manufacturing articles for transportation over their lines or engaging in any business other than that of common carriers.

Unable to reject the burdens while accepting the benefits of Article XVII, the Lackawanna had gone on mining its coal and hauling it under the limited powers granted to it under its charter. It was still mining coal in 1921 and, thanks to the half-forgotten constitution, had come virtually to a dead end. If it stayed in the coal-producing business, it could have no recourse to the statute of 1901. And, except by authorization of the statute of 1901, it could issue no new capital stock.

On February 15, 1921, the Lackawanna petitioned the Interstate Commerce Commission for authority, conditioned on its disposal of its coal properties and acceptance of the Pennsylvania Constitution, to issue additional stock of a par value equal to the amount of its corporate surplus and to distribute such stock pro rata among the stockholders as a dividend. The petition was granted on April 18, 1921. Three days later, the Board of Managers passed a resolution accepting all the provisions of Article XVII. On April 28, 1921, a certified copy of the resolution was filed in Harrisburg.

Sale of the properties had been authorized well in advance of this date by the stockholders, for, as of July 29, 1920, the Board of Managers had passed a resolution ordering the completion of the transfer upon compliance with the Pennsylvania Constitution.

In April 1920, William W. Inglis, at that time vice-president and manager of the coal-mining department of the Lackawanna, had bought the Pine Valley Coal Company, a Pennsylvania corporation. Mr. Inglis and his associates became officers and directors of the Pine Valley Company, changed the name to Glen Alden Coal Company and had the capital stock increased to 850,000 shares.

Capital stock of Glen Alden Coal Company was then offered to the Lackawanna stockholders, each stockholder to receive one share of Glen Alden at a price of $5 for every share of Lackawanna he held. All the stockholders took advantage of the offer, as well they might. On May 10, 1921, rights to purchase stock in Glen Alden were selling on the New York Curb at from $41 to $50. Coal men figured that the new company might be able to pay dividends of about $2 a share, which, at 8 per cent, would make the indicated price of the stock about $25.

On June 15, 1921, the Glen Alden directors authorized President Inglis to offer the Lackawanna $60,000,000 for the road's coal lands and mining business. The railroad accepted the offer, and the contract was approved by the stockholders of the railroad on July 21, 1921.

As of September 1, 1921, the Glen Alden Coal Company took over the Lackawanna coal properties and, by assignment, the sales contract between the railroad and the Delaware, Lackawanna and Western Coal Company. And, as of that date, the Lackawanna Railroad became simply a railroad.

When, on August 25, 1927, the Lackawanna received from Glen Alden Coal Company $58,500,000 par value of Glen Alden bonds, evidencing the amount remaining due under its contract with the railroad to purchase the coal properties for $60,000,000, there was organized the Lackawanna Securities Company to disburse to its stockholders part of the proceeds of the sale of its coal properties. The $58,500,000 par value of Glen Alden bonds were transferred to Lackawanna Securities Company, and the bonds were to constitute the sole assets of the securities company.

Accordingly, the securities company issued its shares to the 6,876 stockholders of the railroad company of record on September 6, 1927, in ratio of one share of securities company stock for each two shares of Lackawanna railroad stock owned, so that the stockholders of the securities company, who were stockholders of the railroad company as well, became the owners of the Glen Alden Coal Company bonds. The sole business activity of the securities company was to collect and distribute to its own stockholders the principal and interest of the coal company's bonds.

The directors of the securities company determined, five years later, on June 30, 1932, to liquidate and distribute the assets to the stockholders, so that payments of principal and interest upon the Glen Alden Coal Company's bonds could be made direct to the beneficial owners of the bonds, without intervention by the securities company. The plan of liquidation was approved by stockholders, August 2, 1932.

The securities company then held $51,000,000 par value of the Glen Alden Coal Company bonds, but no other assets, except a small sum derived from the bonds. The distribution to stockholders had totaled $20 a share, of which $9.92 had been distributed from capital and $10.08 from income.

The bonds delivered by the Glen Alden Coal Company to the Lackawanna Railroad in payment for its coal properties were in denominations of $500,000. Incident to the plan of dissolution of the securities company, however, the Glen Alden Coal Company agreed to exchange its original bonds for bonds of $1,000 denomination, as the means of facilitating the distribution of assets.

The terms decided upon provided that a $1,000 bond would be delivered for each sixteen and one-half shares of securities company stock surrendered for cancellation, while for each fraction of that stock unit, scrip certificates of the Glen Alden Coal Company, likewise bearing interest at 4 per cent and indicating the fractional bond ownership, would be issued upon surrender of stock. The limit date for interest payment on the scrip was September 1, 1934. Stockholders of the securities company, when surrendering stock for bonds, likewise received certificates which entitled them to a final liquidating dividend, provided such were available. The bonds, scrip, and liquidating dividend certificates were distributed to stockholders of record on July 25, 1932. A final liquidation dividend of twenty cents a share was paid on January 30, 1934.

The Supplemental Trust Agreement, which was executed by the railroad, the Glen Alden Coal Company, and The First National Bank of the City of New York, as trustee, also provided that the Glen Alden Coal Company would retire $2,000,000 principal amount of the bonds annually, or expend $1,500,000 annually for the retirement of the bonds (whichever the coal company elected), but that if the coal company did not pay dividends during the years 1932, 1933, and 1934, it was obliged to retire only $1,500,000 principal amount of bonds annually during these years or during any of them in which it did not pay any dividend.

During the period of its activity the securities company disbursed assets consisting of $58,500,000 par value 4 per cent bonds and $9,818,152 interest, a total of $68,318,152, at a cost to stockholders, exclusive of income taxes and other taxes, and insurance, but including all organization, administration, and legal expenses, of only $15,815.84 annually—less than sixteen cents a share. Of this amount $7,362 per annum was for salaries and directors' fees.

19   *Remarkable Achievement*

THE Board of Managers of the Lackawanna on June 25, 1925, on the occasion of Truesdale's retirement, read into the minutes an appreciation that is really a history of his remarkable achievement:

Some eighty years ago the founders of our Company acquired anthracite coal lands in Pennsylvania. In the course of their development, they built and acquired railroads over which to transport the coal to market. Practically all the coal lands were acquired and most of the rail lines comprising our system were built or leased prior to the year 1899. On the second day of March of that year, William Haynes Truesdale became President of our Company and has served continuously until today, when he resigned to become chairman of the board.

Upon assuming charge of the company, he proceeded vigorously to the upbuilding and development of the property, both railroad and mining. From our current earnings, which by exceptionally efficient management were increased yearly, large sums were expended under his personal supervision, with painstaking study and with rare intelligence and broad vision. During his administration our main line of railroad from Hoboken to Buffalo was rock-ballasted and laid with heavy rail, tie plates and screw spikes on creosoted ties, with like work on our branch lines of heavy traffic.

All bridges were rebuilt of steel or concrete. One hundred and eighty-five new stations and freight houses were built, including extensive reconstruction of our Hoboken and Buffalo terminals. Block signals were installed throughout and all important points protected by interlocking plants. Upward of two hundred and sixty grade crossings were eliminated.

New locomotive and car shops were built at East Buffalo and Kingsland. Many miles of second, third and fourth track, including a second tunnel through Bergen Hill, were constructed with many changes of line.

The most notable of the works under his administration were the new construction through the suburban zone and the new lines of railroad built in New Jersey and Pennsylvania known as the New Jersey and Scranton cut-off lines.

Mr. Truesdale directed the same constructive policy to the installations of modern facilities for the economical production of our coal, such as steel and concrete breakers, electrification, and the most improved power-plant, pumping machinery and transportation. He also directed the acquisition of new properties, including our ferry lines, New York and Brooklyn terminals, and Central New York railroads.

With the exception of the Scranton cut-off line, financed by the issue of new stock at par, all such capital expenditures during his administration were from income and aggregate upwards of one hundred and eighty-two million dollars.

The bonded indebtedness of the Company with all its leased companies in the hands of the public is less by sixteen millions than it was in 1899 and totals about thirty-six and a half millions.

Among the corporate changes which were consummated during Mr. Truesdale's administration were the merger into our company of the Bangor and Portland company, the formation by our stockholders of the Delaware, Lackawanna and Western Coal company, which took over the merchandising of our coal, the lease of the Syracuse, Binghamton and New York Railroad company, the issue of a one hundred per cent stock dividend, and the formation of the Glen Alden Coal company and the sale to it of our coal properties. All such changes were largely beneficial to our stockholders.

Mortgages upon many of our leased lands have also been issued to provide bonds to pay our Company for expenditures thereon, many of which are held in our treasury.

Our main lines of railroad are as permanent as modern practice can make them, and our traffic density has increased during the years cited 169 per cent in passenger carrying and 141 per cent in freight. We haul 224 per cent more freight per train and 129 per cent more passengers.

In 1899 anthracite constituted sixty per cent of our freight traffic while today it is less than forty per cent. Of traffic other than such coal we hauled in 1899 five and one half million tons, while in 1924 we hauled seventeen millions.

For the years 1900–1904 our net railway income averaged three and one quarter million dollars while for the years 1920–1924 it averaged eight millions. In the year 1900, $1,834,000 was distributed to our stock-holders in dividends, while in the year 1924, $11,821,754 was so distributed.

In 1900 our book assets were fifty millions and surplus fifteen millions; in 1924 our book assets were two hundred fifty-nine millions and our surplus one hundred and twenty-seven millions. In 1900 we had five and one half millions of distributable surplus; we now have one hundred and twenty-three millions.

In 1899 the division of each dollar received by our company for transportation was 37½ cents to capital; 59½ cents to labor and materials; and three cents for taxes. In 1924 it was 18 cents to capital; 74 cents to labor and materials; and eight cents for taxes.

When Mr. Truesdale became president, the market value of our properties was less than fifty millions. Since then one hundred and ninety-two millions in cash dividends have been declared by our Company and its railroad properties are of the market value of upwards of two hundred and forty millions, while the stock of the two coal companies which now operate and sell the coal we then owned, has a market value of upwards of a hundred and fifty millions more.

These results have been accomplished under federal and state regulation and keen competition from other carriers. On behalf not only of our stockholders and our passenger and freight patrons but also for all our citizens who admire character, integrity, courage, judgment and assiduous devotion to duty, we congratulate you, Mr. President, on your masterly record.

All the board of managers stood up in solemn acquiescence.

William Haynes Truesdale continued as chairman of the board for seven years. He resigned in 1931, at which time the post was abolished. He died of pneumonia at his home in Greenwich, Connecticut, on June 2, 1935, at the age of eighty-four. He had fulfilled the tradition of Lackawanna presidents for longevity.

20 *Man versus Trouble*

JOHN Marcus Davis, who became president of the Lackawanna in 1925, was born to trouble as the sparks fly upward. Most of the big improvements in line and equipment had been completed by that time. The old "Road of Anthracite" no longer had trouble defending its claim to being "the most highly developed railroad in America." Operating revenues were increasing and in 1929 were to reach a high level of $81,743,000. What he could not foresee, and what no amount of railroad engineering could provide against, was the depression that was just over the next hill.

It is one of the most significant things in the Lackawanna's history that the railroad came through that terrible period without a receivership. In 1933 operating revenues hit bottom at $43,339,000. There were indications that they might go lower. But the crux of this story is that they did not. In 1939, before the start of any war boom, they had climbed back to $50,454,000, and a year later, still under peace-time impetus, had reached $51,892,000. Net operating revenue, which was $17,509,000 in 1929, and $3,480,000 in 1933, had reached $6,346,000 in 1940.

Nobody can say that Mr. Davis' years with the Lackawanna were not active nor filled with the discouraging problems that put railroads into the hands of reorganizers all across the country. The Lackawanna seemed to be moving as rapidly as the others toward the point of no return. But that was not the only trouble. Davis had taken over the last of the big improvement projects, the electrification of the Lackawanna's north Jersey suburban service. And that cost $16,000,000.

Davis was born at Palestine, Texas, on November 5, 1871. As a farm boy, his interest was turned to railroads by the building of a section of the Southern Pacific near his father's farm. When he succeeded in wangling a job on a construction train, he knew what he was going to do with the rest of his life. He was educated in private and public schools in Palestine and at Houston Business College.

He started his active railroad career, which was to take him to most centers of the East and Middle West, as stenographer for the Santa Fé at Temple, Texas. He stayed there four years, working as a court stenographer at night.

From 1894 to 1895 he was secretary to the superintendent of the Mexican Central Railroad, Tampico, Mexico. He left there to become chief clerk to the general manager of the Eastern Minnesota Railroad (now the Great Northern) at Duluth, Minnesota. In this job he served five years, leaving it to fit out ten ships for the Union Steamboat Company on the Great Lakes. He was with the Northern Steamship Company of Buffalo for two seasons and in 1903 was superintendent of the Erie and Wyoming Railroad (Erie System) at Dunmore, Pennsylvania, and Hornell, New York. From 1903 to 1906 he was in Superior, Wisconsin, Minot, North Dakota, and St. Paul, Minnesota, as assistant general superintendent and general superintendent of the Central District of the Great Northern. In 1906 he became general superintendent of the Oregon Short Line at Salt Lake City, and left there to go to San Francisco as general superintendent of the Southern Pacific. He was general manager of the Baltimore and Ohio Southwestern from 1914 to 1916 and vice-president in charge of maintenance and operation for the Baltimore and Ohio System from 1916 to 1918.

For a year he served as a member of the U.S. Railroad Association General Managers' Commission and general manager of the Baltimore and Ohio New York terminals. He spent another year in making a survey of New York railroad properties. In 1920 he became advisory chairman of the board and president of Manning, Maxwell and Moore, Inc., manufacturers of railroad machinery. He remained there until his election to the presidency of the Lackawanna in 1925.

When the storm broke, he lived up to his own theory as he had enunciated it in an interview when he took office.*

"A man's progress in life," he had said, "is measured by the degrees of responsibility he is willing to assume. . . . I sometimes think that better executives were made in the days before the telephone and telegraph were invented. In those days men relied on themselves, because they could not telephone a superior officer for orders. . . . The man who can decide without having somebody to help him is a natural born leader. . . . Young men cannot begin too early to make clear-headed decisions. . . ."

His own decision was to increase service, which he did by inaugurating fast-freight runs and improving transfer facilities. He combined and modernized certain sections of the road on which, because the system included a number of short lines, once independent, there was unnecessary duplication. And, finally, he did what could be done about ending a lot of fixed charges on old leases.

It had been the policy of the Lackawanna from the very first to guarantee the dividends on the stock of the roads it leased. In one instance this guaranteed return was as high as 12 per cent.

The job was long and tedious and in some districts, perhaps, a long time getting done. But it indicated some immediate economies. Service, in sections where it was not required at all, was reduced to a minimum. Unused stations were closed. Unused track, where possible, was abandoned. Meanwhile the personnel was beginning to get used to the idea that the Lackawanna, like other railroads, was going to have to pay its own way.

Meanwhile Davis, who, like most Texans, could talk on his feet and loved to do it, went out to convince the public that the railroads might get out of their difficulties if allowed competitive income and freed from strangling regulation. In 1931, before the Central Railway Club of Buffalo, he expressed himself on the depression and showed his stubborn disbelief that it must be considered a permanent condition.

Whether or not the modernization of the Lackawanna's main lines could have been carried out if the depression had come earlier is something for bankers and engineers to argue about during the long

* New York *Post*, Oct. 5, 1925.

winter evenings. The work was well on its way when money became scarce, and nothing much could have been done to stop it. The
main miracle is that the men in charge of running the Lackawanna
brought it to a finish and arranged means of paying for it.

Nobody talks much about the electrification of the north Jersey
suburban service; yet it cost more than either the Clark's Summit–
Hallstead project or the fabulous Jersey cutoff. And it has had an
impact on the lives of more persons than both of them put together.
In a year when there were few major construction projects in the
entire country and virtually no railroad improvements, it suddenly gave the Lackawanna the finest suburban line in the New
York district. The engineering work was in charge of George
Ray. A report on its construction is contained in a letter from Presi-
dent Davis to the executive secretary of the Business Historical
Society, Boston:

. . . The question had been discussed for years by delegations of commuters longing for relief from noise and smoke. A joint committee called
upon the management early in 1928 and demanded electrification, declar-
ing their willingness to pay a reasonable increase in commutation fares.
The project was authorized by the board of managers, March 1928.

Not the least of the problems involved was a survey of all existing wires,
cables, conduits, water and gas mains, sewers—anything that might cause
interference through the absorbing of electric energy from the transmission and contact wires. . . . There were great numbers of readjust-
ments with both individuals and municipalities.

It so happened that the Lackawanna was the first important suburban
electrical installation in America where the railroad did not closely parallel the water level or work on comparatively level ground. After
crossing the meadows west of Hoboken, the Lackawanna takes to the
hills.

Specifications for competitive bids on materials and equipment began
to reach manufacturers in February, 1929. Contracts were let the following August.

The first electrified train was displayed in the Hoboken passenger
terminal August 21 and 22, 1930. Twenty-one thousand four hundred
and forty-one persons came to see it. The first passenger-carrying train,
the President's Special, operated between Hoboken and Montclair,
September 3, 1930. Officers and members of the board, representatives of
companies which supplied materials and equipment, mayors and presi-

dents and secretaries of Chambers of Commerce in towns in the electrified zone, officers and representatives of Public Service companies which had contracted to furnish power, officials of the State Public Utility commission, other state organizations and the press, were aboard.

Thomas A. Edison, whose laboratory and estate are in the region electrified, officiated at the controls as the train left the terminal with two hundred and eighty specially invited passengers.

The first train between Hoboken and South Orange was run on September 22, 1930, with similar fanfare. Oldtime commuters who remembered traveling behind wood-burning engines were among those honored with invitations. First trains between Hoboken and Morristown were run on December 18, 1930, and between Summit and Gladstone on January 6, 1931, all with the same enthusiastic celebrations.

These maiden runs brought out the G.A.R. Vets, and accompanying yarning and oratory. The first electrified train ran between Hoboken and Dover on January 22, 1931. Special souvenir tickets which conducters punched and returned to the holders were sold in quantities. The schools were dismissed throughout the region so the kids could line the right-of-way as the train passed through. There were streamers and flags and bunting and other decorations and brass bands at every stop.

Regular service followed immediately after the opening ceremonies of all sections of the line. Steam trains gave way to electrified trains and were adjusted to the service one at a time, so that if anything should go wrong, one train only and not the entire line, would be tied up.

In this way, full-service load was safely and gradually transmitted to the substations as operating conditions permitted. For the first time in suburban service in America, 3,000 volt direct current is employed. This is believed by the managers to be best suited not only to suburban service but to long-distance main line operation, if ever the time comes when that is installed and electrification is carried across the Delaware and over the Pocono mountains to the anthracite coal fields and Scranton.

The engineers chose to carry the power transmission lines overhead because it is believed impracticable to convey power of such high voltage near the surface of the ground without serious power leakage, and also as a matter of safety in a highly populated region.

The company originally contemplated the construction of a plant of its own for the manufacture of power, but finally decided to confine its activities to transportation. Contracts were concluded with Public Service companies serving that region.

The railroad constructed five strategically located substations for the receipt of alternating current of varying voltages where it is transformed and rectified to the required three thousand volts direct current and sent out over the transmission system for use by the trains as needed.

Seventy miles of road, carrying 160 miles of track, are included in the project. Multiple unit equipment, one motor car and one trailer car constituting a unit, is employed in trains of from two to twelve cars. All steel motor coaches seat eighty-four, trailer coaches from seventy-eight to eighty-two.

The speed of the train accelerates each second at a rate of 1½ miles per hour on level track, which is about four times as fast as steam trains get under way. If the engineer removes his hand from the power control lever while the train is in motion, power immediately cuts off and the train stops automatically.

Old automatic semaphore signals have been replaced by new color-light signals which change more quickly and permit operations of faster trains at closer intervals with safety. They can be detected by engineers in bright sunlight for thousands of feet and, as far as the alignment of track permits, on the darkest nights. Steam whistle and bell have been succeeded by pneuphonic horn which is as penetrating but less shrill. These horns throw their warning both forward and back and protect the public when the trains are backing as well as when moving forward.

The use of 3,000 volt direct current in railroad suburban service is an innovation in America. Rectifiers in railroad electrification are not uncommon, but those in major stations of the Lackawanna are the first in America and the largest in the world to be operated by a direct current of this voltage in railroad service.

The time of moving a commuter between his home and office has, of course, been materially reduced. The average reduction is probably twenty per cent or more. Other advantages are the smoothness with which the trains accelerate and come to a stop, and the increased amount and improved diffusion of light.

During peak-hour periods, traffic streams through the Hoboken station at a rate of about three hundred persons per minute. And this rate will increase steadily. About one million two hundred and fifty thousand persons live in this sector of New Jersey, large portions of which are only sparsely populated.

There were other considerable improvements in the road during the Davis regime: a new three-track lift bridge over the Hackensack River on the Morristown line, replacing an old one that had to be opened for tugs and other small craft; a new bascule bridge over the relocated channel of the Buffalo River; extensions and improvements of Hoboken terminal facilities; two concrete bridges of unusual span length, one at Paterson Junction, New Jersey, and one a mile east of Denville, New Jersey; numerous grade separation projects growing out of the electrification.

Davis went on through all the troubled time, serene and undisturbed. He retired in January, 1941, almost a year before the Second World War overtook the United States. He had been in office fifteen years and seven months. During that time he had seen the bottom drop out of everything. He had seen the Lackawanna's operating revenues cut virtually in two. In 1929 the earned net operating income had been $17,509,000; he saw it go down to $3,480,000 in 1933 and $2,510,000 in 1938. But he had seen it climb back to reach a total of $6,346,000 in 1940. He lived long enough after his retirement, as a member of the board and of the executive committee, to see a return to normal conditions and a new hope.

He died on March 2, 1944, in New York City. He was seventy-two years old.

21   *One More War*

THE Second World War was well on its way when John M. Davis relinquished the leadership of the Lackawanna Railroad. The Low Countries had been invaded; France had collapsed; the British Army had been evacuated from Dunkerque; the Battle of Britain was going on, with all the odds in favor of the Germans. The impact of these disasters was already being felt in the United States. Men of foresight—and there were still some men of foresight in America—considered that we might be lucky to keep out of it another year, after which nobody was prepared to say what might happen to the railroads or to the country.

Posed with this problem, the Board of Managers elected to the presidency on January 1, 1941, William White, who, since 1938, had been vice-president and general manager of the Virginian Railway. Mr. White, at forty-three, thus became the youngest president of a Class I railroad in the United States.

Twenty-five years of experience with the Erie had acquainted him with all the difficulties that were likely to beset a railroad of the Lackawanna's character—up to that time. He had a broad general training, and he had stamina, both of which he was presently going to need.

The road, of course, had never been so well prepared for an emergency, but, with a canny sense of trouble ahead, he made it better. Through 1941 all heavy freight locomotives were reconditioned. New rail was laid in anticipation of heavy traffic. And an order was placed for 1,250 new boxcars to be delivered early in 1942.

At the end of the year the country was at war. An Office of Defense Transportation had been set up. And the new president was up to his neck in problems for which neither his experience nor that of anybody else had provided ready answers.

William White, born in Midland Park, New Jersey, on February 3, 1897, had gone into the railroad business straight from high school at the age of sixteen. His first job was clerk in the office of the auditor of freight accounts for the Erie Railroad in New York. After a few months he was transferred to the office of the super-intendent of the New York, Susquehanna and Western Railroad (an Erie subsidiary) in Jersey City and after three years moved back to the office of the vice-president of the Erie in New York.

In December, 1916, he was assigned to the vice-president as secretary, which post he held until our entry into the First World War. At the start of Federal control of the railroads he acted as secretary to the assistant director of the Eastern Region, and sec-retary of the New York District conference committee. Then he enlisted as an infantryman and served for two years, being dis-charged as regimental sergeant major.

On his return from war service he was appointed office manager of the operating department of the Ohio region of the Erie Rail-road with headquarters in Youngstown, Ohio. In January, 1923, he was promoted to trainmaster and transferred to Marion, Ohio, which he left, after a year, for a similar post at Huntington, Indiana.

In January, 1927, he was made terminal superintendent of the Mahoning division of the Erie and a month later became superinten-dent of the division.

In September, 1929, Mr. White became assistant general manager of the western district and in 1934 was appointed assistant to the vice-president in charge of operation at Cleveland. In April, 1936, he went back to New York as general manager of the eastern district.

Mr. White went to the Virginian Railway in 1938 as vice-president and general manager and for three years had an important hand in the operation of one of the most unusual railroads in the country. The Virginian is a new railroad, as railroads go in the United States. It was built just before the First World War "all of a piece," on the highest standards of the day and without reference to cost. Its purpose in the end was to do, as cheaply as possible, the specific job of hauling coal from the West Virginia fields to tidewater at Norfolk, Virginia. It has been one of the most profitable of American railroads.

A step from such a line to the Lackawanna implied some changes. The Lackawanna, to begin with, was one of the oldest roads in the United States. It was a combination of numerous short lines welded after many years into an integral system. It handled all the varieties of traffic that may lie between anthracite coal and suburban passenger service.

On the other hand, there were also some similarities. Ignoring what the Lackawanna might have been before 1900, it had certainly become a road of high physical standards. It was good and getting better and developing a reputation among travelers all out of proportion to the length of its track. Less spectacularly, it was beginning to get the fast-freight business between New York and Buffalo. All in all, Mr. White was taking over a job with which he was eminently familiar.

One of the first indications of what the new war was going to mean to the railroads came with the rationing of rubber. Truck transport continued, of course, but numerous fly-by-night companies that had been hauling coal went out of business almost immediately, and the tonnage they had handled went back to the railroads. Within a few months Lackawanna freight agents estimated the increased coal business at 14 per cent of the total.

The volume of freight traffic in 1942 set a new record for the road. Passenger traffic was at the highest level since 1926. It was estimated that with fewer locomotives and fewer train miles the average net tons per train increased 23.9 per cent and the average number of passengers per train 29.20.

Fortunately some of the new equipment previously ordered was delivered that year: 400 50-ton box cars, 250 50-ton gondola cars, six 500-ton covered barges, nine 400-ton covered barges, seven 400-ton lighters, two 450-ton lighters, and one 25-ton locomotive crane. That was to be just about the end of equipment delivery until after the war. But construction work went on: sundry track extensions serving industries or government projects at Chatham, Montville, Harrison, Delawanna, Kearney, and Jersey City, New Jersey, at Danville and Scranton, Pennsylvania, and at Baldwinsville, Binghamton, Syracuse, Johnson City, Brisbin, East Buffalo, and South Brooklyn, New York; installations to serve forty-three new industries along the Lackawanna right-of-way; storage facilities furnished by the government at Dover, New Jersey, and Binghamton and Depew, New York.

In 1943 thirty-six new war industries were opened up along the line, and by the end of the year gross revenues had reached the 1929 high. Things had changed, however. With approximately the same gross revenue in 1929 and 1943, the 1929 earnings on a share of common stock had been $7.90, as against $2.78 in 1943. Operating costs were about the same, but taxes were not.

As a result of a decision by the U.S. Court of Appeals, on April 2, 1942, that the Delaware, Lackawanna and Western Railroad Company was not obligated to pay Federal income taxes assessed against three of its lessor companies, suits were brought by these lines against the company. To adjust the difficulty, plans were drawn for merging the lessor companies—New York, Lackawanna and Western Railway Company, the Morris and Essex Railroad Company, the Lackawanna Railroad Company of New Jersey, and the Utica, Chenango and Susquehanna Valley Railway Company—and purchase of the Valley Railroad Company. Agreements were prepared for approval by the Interstate Commerce Commission.

At the request of the War Department, the Lackawanna accepted sponsorship of a Railway Shop Battalion, Transportation Corps, for which it furnished officer-personnel. At the completion of its training in the Army Service Forces Unit training center in Louisiana, this battalion was given the highest rating of any unit that had gone through the camp. The war, meanwhile, had made great inroads on personnel. The loss of 1,519 employees to the armed forces was beginning to be felt more and more as traffic increased and replacement became more and more difficult.

Nineteen forty-four was a record year in many ways and for many reasons. The volume of freight-ton-miles and passenger-miles exceeded all previous experience. Wages and taxes hit a new peak simultaneously. Man-power shortage and the lack of materials to keep equipment in repair became a serious problem, just as the absence of coastwise shipping and the curtailment of motor hauling by rationing and the increasing tempo of the war on all fronts put a new transportation burden on the rails.

That year Mr. White sounded a bit of common-sense warning in the middle of wild whoopee. He said:

As a result of the unprecedented volume of traffic that has come to them during the past few years, the railroads have shown relatively favorable operating results. . . . This in spite of being obliged to pay the highest wages and the highest taxes in their history and in spite of other increases in their operating costs.

However, the influence of constantly increasing traffic has spent itself, and for each month since June, 1943, railway net earnings have shown a constant and rapid downward trend. Railroad (all railroad) net income dropped from $902,000,000 in 1942 to $660,000,000 in 1944.

The railroads have never been misled into believing that their recent period of relative prosperity could be other than temporary. For that reason they have endeavored to take the best possible advantage of it by using it as a means for preparing themselves for the conditions with which they will be confronted after the war. . . .

They see at least one certainty. They know the development which the war has brought in air navigation. They know of the plans for vast postwar expansion of civilian aviation as announced by the Civil Aeronautics Administration of the Department of Commerce. They are familiar with the plans of the Maritime Commission for the construction of cargo vessels. They are acquainted with the many plans that are now being pressed for extensive highway, superhighway and interior waterway improvements. As a result of these developments, it will not be long before the rail carriers will be compelled to face the keenest competition from the other transportation agencies that they have ever experienced. . . .

President White's personal view of the future and what ought to be done about it was reflected in the purchase during 1945 of two 2,700-horsepower Diesel-electric freight helper locomotives, four 4,050-horsepower Diesel-electric road freight locomotives, and ten 1,000-horsepower Diesel-electric switching locomotives— certainly unusual equipment for the "Road of Anthracite."

The merger of the leased lines, initiated in 1942, was completed in that year. Of eighteen lessor companies, thirteen were merged and the property of one acquired by purchase, so that only four small segments of the road remained on a lease basis. These four companies were not included in the original merger plan; three of them because no Federal income-tax problem was involved, and one because the tax problem was minor.

"The effect of the completion of the merger program," the president reported, "was a reduction in net fixed charges of $1,153,570, so that at the end of 1945, net fixed charges on obligations issued or assumed as part of the merger . . . were $4,960,269 annually." The Lackawanna Company paid all Federal taxes owed by the lessor companies and fixed interest from the date when rental under the lease was last paid. Taxes, $9,198,521. Fixed interest, $3,803,099.

The next year, 1946, was theoretically the year in which the United States, recovering from the war, was getting down to business. To a railroad man it might well have been one of shocking discouragement. Out of a gross revenue of $69,481,551 that year, the company was able to extract a net of only $36,216. *Vide* Annual Report for 1946.

This slight net income was possible only because of a carry-back tax credit of $933,531 and because we were favored with reasonably good operating weather. Except for anthracite coal, we handled the greatest volume of freight traffic of any peacetime year. . . .

Strikes! Two bituminous coal strikes, a truck strike in New York City and vicinity, strikes in the automobile, steel, meat-packing, electrical supply, and other industries. And the first nationwide railroad strike since the shopmen's strike of 1922 and the first since the enactment of the Railway Labor Act of 1926. . . . Freight-car shortage, the first since 1923. A record grain crop, a heavy volume of less carload freight, strikes, the five-day week, and a deficiency in total railroad ownership caused this shortage. Freight cars are still operated in a pool, without regard to car service rules, and the Interstate Commerce Commission has ordered thousands of cars moved empty to the West, largely to move the grain crop. Our company, while not found to be deficient in ownership by any formula used, nevertheless suffered seriously. . . .

All these things unbalanced production lines of the country and had an adverse effect on railroad operations. . . . In the final analysis it would appear that the outlook . . . is dependent entirely upon labor. Should production of goods be not curtailed and costs not materially increased, our company may look forward to an improvement in net earnings. But in order to insure an adequate return, it is our opinion that there must be some further increase in freight rates and passenger fares. There is, however, a limit to which freight rates and passenger fares can be increased because of competition from other forms of transportation that receive sudsidies at the expense of taxpayers.

The following year was one of record-breaking freight-carrying performance. Passenger traffic had dropped off considerably, but was still heavier than it had been in the years immediately preceding the war.

The net earnings for 1947, too, were more encouraging, a total of $3,257,326 against the $36,216 of 1946. The cost of doing business, however, continued to rise, and the freight-car shortage was the worst in twenty-five years.

The last two of the small leased lines of the system were merged that year, making a further reduction in fixed charges. The only lease remaining in force was the one with the Hoboken Ferry Company, of which the Lackawanna owned all the stock.

"As a result of these two mergers and the purchase of bonds and former leased line stocks," Mr. White mentioned, "the net fixed charges, December 31, 1947, on outstanding bonds were reduced to $4,593,269 on an annual basis, and the contingent interest was reduced to $571,115 annually. This compares with net annual fixed charges on December 31, 1940, of $6,336,319."

The business of the war was not yet done, and the latest manifestation of it was devious and confusing. And concerning this, too, the president made a report to the stockholders:

Early in World War II a railroad committee was organized at the request of Director Eastman, Office of Defense Transportation (and with written approval of the Department of Justice) empowered to act upon all proposals concerning freight rates and traffic practices of an emergency nature presented by governmental agencies. This committee functioned throughout the war in respect to all freight-rate reductions requested by the government.

Many items of war materials were handled on government bills of lading at rates substantially lower than those paid by the general public. The Department of Justice now alleges that the functioning of the very railroad committee set up at the request of the government itself and which the Department of Justice approved in writing constitutes an unlawful conspiracy in respect to railroad rates on war materials.

The railroads have been forced to set up an organization of law, traffic, and accounting representatives who will have to devote substantially their entire time to the defense of these cases. The total amount of money involved in the claims made by the Department of Justice is not known, but it is estimated at not less than three billion dollars.

Thus, after the utmost cooperation with the government at the government's request, and after making concessions in rates to government agencies below those charged to the general public, after paying excess profits taxes on war revenues and earning an average return of less than five per cent on the value of their property during the war years, and after handling the greatest volume of freight and passenger traffic in the history of the country in a manner that gained unstinted praise, the railroads are forced to defend themselves, at great expense, against claims by the Department of Justice alleging overcharges! Such a government attitude is difficult of comprehension.

Despite such annoyances, the good years continued. Gross revenue in 1948 was the highest in the history of the road; the net income highest since 1929. But even so the return on investment was only 4.28 per cent.

For the third time the government was forced to intervene in a labor dispute. Wages and other operating costs continued to rise. The competition between the railroads and other forms of transportation developed, as President White had prophesied that it would back in the beginning of his regime.

He was not too gloomy in his estimate of the future, but he was realistic.

"The postwar boom in business," he said, "lasted three years. Railroads participated in handling this large volume, but did not participate in large earnings. This paradoxical situation is portrayed by the rate of return on investment in transportation property less depreciation, which for all Class I railroads was 2.75 per cent in 1946; 3.41 per cent in 1947, and 4.38 per cent in 1948. For our company the rates of return were 1.98 per cent, 3.20 per cent, and 4.28 per cent respectively.

"Since 1939 labor cost has increased 93 per cent; material and fuel, 123 per cent; freight rates have increased 49 per cent; passenger fares, 30 per cent.

"As business volume recedes . . . railroads are caught in the vise of high cost and subsidized competition. . . . Railroads should have been permitted to have large earnings during the postwar boom while heavy volume was available. . . . Measured in terms of what the dollar will buy, the net income of 1948 was less than one-quarter of that of 1929.

". . . Because of rising prices it takes many more dollars than original cost to replace worn-out facilities. Hence depreciation reserves thus set up are inadequate for the funds needed today for identical replacements only, to say nothing of improvements required to keep abreast of competition and to reduce operating costs."

An encouraging feature of the year's proceedings was the report that a number of new passenger cars would be delivered in 1949, the first in more than twenty years.

Morale, for some reason or another, continued to be high.

Part III: LEGEND AND FACT

22 *Phoebe Snow*

In the vaudeville of our innocent childhood there was one joke that never failed to get a rousing hand, the one about the little boy who was asked to name the two most famous women in history and promptly answered, "My Mamma's Mamma and Phoebe Snow." Any way you take it, that was less of a joke than contemporary critics seemed to think. But thousands of people remember Phoebe Snow better today than they do the Gibson Girl or Anna Held or Little Annie Rooney or Amelia Jenks Bloomer or Maxine Elliott or the Cherry Sisters.

Phoebe Snow came onto the American scene for the first time in 1900, when the country was just beginning to realize that such innovations as the telephone, electric light, the solo saxophone, and display advertising had come to stay. Nobody had ever heard of her. Her family tree is still the subject of considerable discussion. But suddenly there she was, a dream of loveliness, suavity, poise, and shining cleanliness, smiling down on the home-bound office workers of a hundred cities from a streetcar advertising card. Several thousand grubby men ran fingers around inside their wilting collars and attempted to straighten their wet little bow ties. Several thousand stenographers, wriggling in moist corsets, gazed despairingly on Phoebe's cool aloofness. Everybody who looked at her might be sweating pearls, but not Phoebe. She was not only clean. She was completely comfortable in unrumpled linens, gleaming white and sharply starched. Not a bang—not a single hair—was plastered against her alabaster brow. And yet, wonder of wonders, she had not—as one might think—just emerged from a leisurely bath and toilette in an ice house. Right here in the large print you could read about it. Phoebe Snow was just finishing a long, summertime trip on a railroad train:

Here is the maiden all in lawn
Who boarded the train one early morn
    That runs on the Road of Anthracite
And when she left the train that night
She found, to her surprised delight
    Hard coal had kept her dress still white.

The meter of that introduction may have carried the suggestion that Phoebe was related to "the maiden all forlorn who milked the cow with the crumpled horn" or, more recently, to "the maiden of Spotless Town." But presently the bulletins of Phoebe's progress were as personal and individual as herself. They went something like this—scores of them:

Says Phoebe Snow
About to go
Upon a trip
    To Buffalo
"My gown stays white
From morn till night
Upon the Road of Anthracite."

And about that time the car-card readers began to realize that the Lackawanna Railroad was presenting Phoebe in a bid for patronage on the novel plan of public service. Phoebe's smile and her crisp, white look were no accident. They were a calculated lure. Phoebe was out to make men forget the recognized verities of railroad travel, that no matter how the car window stuck, no matter how airtight the unventilated Pullman might be, the traveler could always get a cinder in his eye and pick up enough soot to look like the end man in a minstrel show. And that any railroad management might think the matter important enough to let her talk about it in the car ads seemed to give promise of a new day.

Her laundry bill
For fluff and frill
Miss Phoebe finds
  Is nearly nil
It's always light
Though in gowns of white
She rides the Road of Anthracite.

Not so long ago advertising men were debating the value of rhymed ads. This sort of appeal to the consumer, the pundits agreed, was frivolous, not to say childish. People read the rhymes, and memorized them, and repeated them, and made parodies on them, but the deep significance of the copywriter's message was lost in the general amazement at his verbal adroitness. Well, maybe. This is no place for an argument about advertising techniques. But at the turn of the century the United States east of the Rockies suddenly became aware of the Delaware, Lackawanna and Western Railroad. And nobody who lived in those days has ever been able to forget it since.

For the purpose of the record, one may take a look at Chicago in the early 1900's. The day of high-speed Diesels was still far ahead, and the memory of the little tin teapots that hauled the pioneers west was not too far behind, but the town certainly had plenty of connections with New York. The Lake Shore and Michigan Southern—one day to be known as the New York Central—had daily trains running somewhere in that direction. So did the Pennsylvania, and the Baltimore and Ohio, and the Nickel Plate, and the Grand Trunk. The Erie had been shuttling between Lake Michigan and the Hudson River for years and years. But after the arrival of Phoebe Snow nobody in Chicago—nobody in the Middle West, especially the younger generation—had any recollection of that. To the readers of the car cards there was only one railroad with a line to Manhattan.

Phoebe Snow did other things besides keeping herself clean while riding on the "Road of Anthracite." When her immaculate figure had been presented in a great variety of poses by Penrhyn Stanlaus and numerous other popular illustrators, the ad-writing poet put

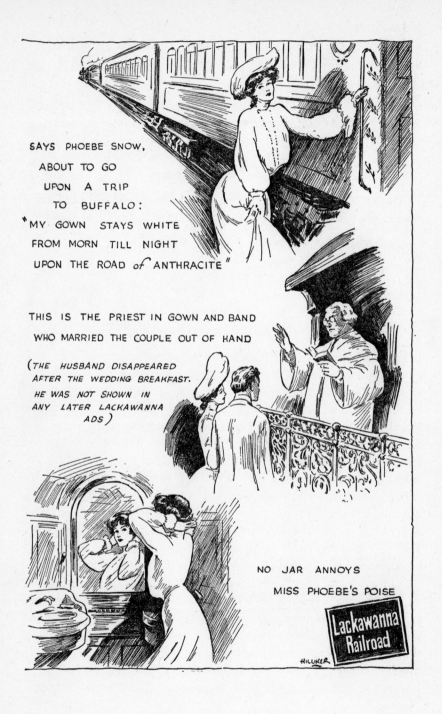

a new string on his harp. He gave the girl a chance to look around
a bit:

> It's time to go
> With Phoebe Snow
> Where banks of rhododendron blow
> In pink and white
> On every height
> Along the Road of Anthracite.

And as summer warmed up, Miss Snow discovered another Lackawanna attraction for which no charge was included in her fare:

> It's time to go
> Where records show
> It's cooler ten degrees or so
> By Fahrenheit
> Each Summer night
> Along the Road of Anthracite.

Each new phase of Phoebe's activity was presented in detail, with
eye-stopping examples of the country's top poster art, which certainly had come a long way from the woodcuts that portrayed the
Lackawanna's pot-stacked engines on the timetables of the seventies.
Phoebe in the beginning had been merely a pleasant figure posing
on the lower step of a railroad car to display the whiteness of her
frock. (The comedian Pete Dailey was widely quoted for his observation that she had not got off the step nor changed her costume
for two months.) But there was no kinship between a dressmaker's
dummy and the glamour girl that Phoebe shortly turned out to be.
She was easily the most traveled woman in the world. Until
Federal control in the First World War forced the railroads to burn
bituminous coal and made it impossible for her any longer to ride the
"Road of Anthracite," she defended her record. No other lovely
gadabout—not even one in a black dress—had ever got around so
far or so continuously. And she had legs, although in that period
nobody was allowed to mention such matters; but, after a while,
she was permitted to exercise them in other ways besides walking
between the baggage car and the observation platform of the Lackawanna Limited. Her eager public found out that she played tennis,

golfed, swam, bicycled, rode horseback, paddled a canoe, and otherwise conducted herself as a healthy and ornamental outdoor girl. She carried on these activities, of course, in resorts reached quickly—and spotlessly—on the "Road of Anthracite."

It is likely that, although the posters show her always with a sort of portmanteau and an overnight case, she must have been accompanied by an imposing assortment of wardrobe trunks. Phoebe Snow had a complete outfit of clothes for everything from "Looking at Delaware Water Gap" to "Retiring in an Electrically Lighted Pullman Sleeping Berth." And every time she changed her dress, her envious followers talked about it.

By the end of 1907 Phoebe Snow was a personality definitely established in the American imagination. There were continuous pleasantries about her in vaudeville, little articles about her in the magazines, and she made an occasional appearance in the changing cartoons of the day. Her diary, if anybody had kept one for her, would be filled with somewhat familiar stories, some of which may have been true. Like many another vivid but fictitious character, she had a heavy fan mail. The railroad and the advertising agency received in her name gifts of Thanksgiving turkeys, samples of prize-winning tomato preserves, pleas for charity, free horoscopes, and proposals of marriage from lonesome homesteaders in North Dakota. She got several letters from people named Snow who wondered whether or not they might claim relationship. (". . . Let's see, there was Captain Matthias Alfred Snow who came to Massachusetts Colony in 1747 in the brig 'Alcibiades,' and he had a daughter called Philomena, which might have been a misspelling of Phoebe. . . .") And there was the customary run of letters from better identified crackpots demanding money or threatening exposure. Anyway it became pretty obvious to everybody connected with the Lackawanna that to a celebrity-worshiping public Phoebe Snow was a living, breathing person.

It is true that Phoebe's influence on contemporary life, aside from railroad travel, may have been neither vital nor lasting. But at the peak of her popularity the current equivalent of bobby-soxers were aping her manners, while their elder sisters copied her hairdo. In a modest way she set the style for a large portion of the female populace. The world was filled with Phoebe Snow frocks and Phoebe

Snow hats and Phoebe Snow handbags and shoes and umbrellas and corsets and shirtwaists, not to mention lines of Phoebe Snow tennis and boating and horseback-riding attire and high-necked bathing suits that would shock the modesty of nobody on the "Road of Anthracite" or off it.

Hardly a year went by without some variation of the Phoebe Snow theme in the vaudeville reviews. The central figure in the first one was to be confused with the young woman she portrayed in the skit for a long time to come—despite her well-publicized maiden name, Janet Allen. (She is now Mrs. James J. Walker, widow of New York's ebullient mayor.)

"I do remember," she recalls, "that we used a set with back-drop, showing the rear platform of the last car. There were six girls dressed in uniforms made by the tailor who made the railroad uniforms: Conductor (straight); Baggage Man (Irish); Engineer, (slight character); Porter and Chef (blackface); and Newsboy (fresh kid).

"We required the girls to sing, dance, and read lines I do not now remember. As Phoebe Snow, I wore a white suit, hat, and shoes, with a large corsage of purple violets. There was an opening number, two numbers with the girls, a trio with the porter and chef, and a solo, 'I Like Your Way,' Jim's number [Mayor Walker's], written for 'the Duke of Duluth.' One of the numbers was called, 'Hang Your Little Lantern Out,' in which we used regulation trainmen's lanterns."

Janet Allen's Phoebe Snow show was another factor that gave the Penrhyn Stanlaus girls a semblance of flesh and blood. The Walker skit was the most pretentious of the series that moved on and off the American stage for years. Some of the later exhibits—along about the time the Germans moved into Liège—were little more than ballet numbers with a principal in a while lawn costume, assisted by coryphees wearing conductors' caps, and swinging lanterns. By that time Phoebe was ready to go into retirement anyway, although nobody seemed conscious of it. Her clothes had altered with the times, but her face had not. In 1917 she was still as young and fresh looking as she had been when she first started to ride the "Road of Anthracite" in 1900.

Miss Snow came partly out of her retirement in 1942. The line's coal cars were painted with the lettering "The Road of Anthracite," and the boxcars decorated with "Lackawanna, The Route of Phoebe Snow."

Then, in November, 1949, Phoebe—none the worse for thirty-odd years—came back to the car cards and newspaper advertisements and the interested regard of a new generation of flappers. One historical-minded columnist on the Scranton *Times* reprinted the favored jape of the old Keith circuit: "She came clean from Hoboken." And so she did. Wherever she had been cloistering herself during two wars and two decades of uneasy peace, she was still as spotless as she was ageless.

She came, this time, with suitable fanfare and a train of her own, a new million-dollar Diesel affair that she should have looked upon with considerable amazement. If only because it was the most recent specimen to leave the car shops, it was, on the day of its inauguration, the most advanced piece of transportation equipment in the world, complete with really comfortable seats, roomy dining cars and lounges, through sleeping cars to Chicago, and power enough in the triple-unit Diesel engine to clip more minutes off the shortest route between New York and Buffalo.

Officials of the Lackawanna rode the Phoebe Snow Streamliner north from Hoboken on the initial trip. With them were a few aging advertising men who had promoted Phoebe's popularity at the turn of the century. Also in the party was Mrs. Marion Gorsch, nee Marion Murray, Penrhyn Stanlaus' model for the original Miss Snow. Newspapers from New York to Chicago pointed up the event with sundry quotations of the old jingles, some of which seemed almost undated:

> Each passing look
> At nook or brook
> Unfolds a flying picture book. . . .

Or

> Like aeroplanes
> My favorite trains
> O'ertop the lofty mountain chains. . . .

And

Each cut and fill
'Cross dale and hill
Has made *The Shortest* shorter still.

But the members of the inaugural party did not have to be told
that Phoebe Snow's new public was likely to be puzzled by the
climax of the resurrected jingles. As they lay back on foam-rubber
cushions and watched telegraph posts slipping by at an easy eighty
miles an hour and breathed the clean, invigorating air supplied
by the air-conditioning system, the truth was obvious: Phoebe
Snow was back to stay—but this time because of oil instead of anthracite.

One anecdote of Phoebe Snow that has stayed in the memory of
railroad men concerns William H. Truesdale, president of the
Lackawanna between 1899 and 1925, Frederick D. Underwood,
contemporaneous president of the Erie, and Phoebe Smith, a Jamai-
can-born Negress who acted as a sort of janitress in the Lackawanna executive offices at 140 Cedar Street, New York. Phoebe, a
large, cheerful and midnight-black woman, never got into the car
cards, but she was the only Phoebe the railroad personnel cared
about. She was on friendly terms with everybody in the building
from the president to the office boy.

Truesdale and Underwood were close friends and frequently had
luncheon together. One day, as they were leaving the Lackawanna
offices, they met Phoebe Smith coming in.

"Good morning, Mr. Truesdale," greeted Phoebe.

"Good morning, Phoebe," responded Truesdale.

"Good Lord!" said Underwood, "Is that Phoebe Snow?"

"That's her," agreed Truesdale, "but she just got off the Erie."

The musical efforts provoked by Phoebe Snow, such as "Hang
Your Little Lantern Out," were topical and went the way of the
shows in which they were offered. Some, such as "The Phoebe
Snow Intermezzo," by a long-forgotten composer, never shared to
any great extent in the popularity of their subject.

A more recent offering is that of Louis F. Ludwig, librettist and
composer.

Phoebe Snow Is Back Again*

Many years ago, there was a Phoebe Snow
    Who rode up and down the Lackawanna.
She was a lady fair with that certain air
    No wonder all eyes were upon her.

She's here again today, but in a different way
    That is why it makes us feel so all aglow
And you'll get to know her, too, for she will be taking you
    On the shortest route to Buffalo.

Chorus

Phoebe Snow is back again
And now she is a streamlined train
With all new cars
As bright as stars
We know you'll want to ride again.

She has all modern coaches and diner
The last word in comfort
Nothing could be finer.
Phoebe Snow is back again
She'll make your travel dreams come true.

* By permission of Louis F. Ludwig, copyright holder.

23   *Oil Painting*

As you come down the hill from Clark's Summit and make the turn toward the Delaware, Lackawanna and Western's Scranton station, you see little that suggests the early life of Slocum's Hollow. Out beyond the car window on your left stretches the mass of brick and stone and iron of a modern industrial city. There are zigzags of white road on the soft gray and green of the faraway mountains, and breaker towers in the nearer distance.

None of these things except the mountains was here ninety-five years ago, which may have been a great blessing, but there were other objects that in almost any generation would have been considered no more beautiful: in the middle distance a smoke-plumed roundhouse that was actually round, and an arc of iron track curving dully through a raw, fresh cut; an unpaved wagon road meandering out through the dust toward a half-veiled settlement; cut-over land with the stumps still showing in the foreground, and beyond, bold against the bluish slope of the hills, a tall church spire.

There was little enough in this prospect to delight the eye of the beholder or to inspire the tremendous talent of one of America's great painters. Looking across the same landscape today, one might doubt that George Innes ever saw it, except for the spire. That is still where he saw it, still dominant, still the one permanent thing in a changed new world.

George D. Phelps, the first president of the Delaware, Lackawanna and Western Railroad, was generally considered by contemporary

184

opinion as erratic, but he deserves to be remembered through the years as a patron of art.

Phelps may have been given an insight and taste denied lesser men, but in any case he was the first person in the world to pick the Lackawanna roundhouse as the subject for a fine oil painting. There was much talk in New York about the rising young artist named George Innes, and, as he became more and more convinced that people outside of Scranton should have the privilege of seeing the roundhouse as he saw it, Phelps decided to commission George Innes. Nothing but the best!

Despite the fact that success was beginning to knock at the door loudly enough to be heard, Innes and his wife were just about flat broke. The debts of some lean years were just getting paid off. Therefore, when President Phelps outlined what he wanted done and offered a flat fee of $75 for the doing of it, the artist accepted.

Innes was not too modest to know that he rated a much larger payment than $75, but he seems to have understood something about Mr. Phelps. The railroad man, whose daily life had nothing at all to do with art, actually thought he was offering a top price, and, for anybody except an Innes, it probably was just that. At any rate, that much money would buy a lot of subsistence in New York in the fifties and it was money ready at hand.

Not trusting some parts of the New Jersey railroad system, Innes made the trip to Scranton by stagecoach. The journey took nearly four days each way, and the stopovers at night were pretty rugged. On the last leg of the trip into Scranton, Innes discovered that somebody had stolen his bag, and he had to write to his wife for funds. Meanwhile he lived as frugally as he could on credit at "The Wyoming House."

The picture, on which he obviously put in considerable time and effort, is simply described in the catalogue of the National Gallery of Art:

View of a wide, flat valley with a broad band of undulating hills in the background. Roundhouse in middle distance to right of center. From it tracks wind into foreground and to left. In immediate foreground at left, footpath leads to right, at the side of which a boy with straw hat and bright red vest lies watching a train making its way around the bend at the right.

This gives you the bare bones of the work, although it conveys nothing of the wonder of the scene, interpreted obviously through the boy's eyes. There is amazing and mysterious distance in the picture, and the lighting has robbed nearly all the unbeautiful foreground of its ugliness.

It is fair to mention, however, that there are certain inaccuracies of detail. For instance, in 1854, when George Innes first laid eyes on this scene, there was no such business in front of the roundhouse as the finished picture showed. George Innes, Jr., his son, comments on this in his book, *Life, Art and Letters of George Innes* *:

. . . There was in reality only one track at the time running into the roundhouse. . . . The president of the road insisted on having four or five painted in, easing his conscience by explaining that the road would eventually have them.

Pop protested but the president was adamant and there was a family to support, so the tracks were painted in.

There were some other points that aroused considerable argument before the canvas was accepted. The Lackawanna owned three locomotives, and Phelps wanted them all in the picture, a sort of family group around the circular shed. This time Innes said no; he would go home first. He would draw one locomotive, and he would indicate the presence of others by means of smoke wisps in the distance. Phelps reluctantly agreed, but he maintained his artistic principles by demanding that the letters "D. L. & W." appear prominently on the locomotive.

When you think about it, this, too, was a pictorial untruth. The locomotives were not labeled "D. L. & W." but "Simon DeWitt," "W. R. Humphrey," and "G. W. Scranton." Mr. Innes did not know any of these gentlemen, and he did not care whether they were being slighted or not, but the idea of letters in the middle of his fine painting drove him into a rage. The world might never have seen the picture, had it not been for his wife, who did not think the point worth $75 worth of argument. The letters were painted in, Phelps accepted the canvas, and handed over the $75.

Then, apparently, the president's idea of advertising in the modern way got sidetracked by more pressing matters. The picture disap-

---

* The Century Company, New York, 1917.

peared, and for the next thirty years less is known of it than of George Phelps, which is little enough.

The denouement of the story is one of those impossible twists that no magazine editor would countenance in a fiction story. Along about 1892, the artist and his wife were browsing about a junk shop in Mexico City when, amid a debris of old china, ancient tools, and office furniture, they discovered an oil painting in a broken gilt frame. Innes turned it over, took it to the light and looked at it. . . .

The shopkeeper knew nothing of its origin. He had not been able to find any signature on it, he said. Most likely it was an advertisement for some railroad up north. But it was obviously an old picture—look at the engine. Where did they have engines like that nowadays? And the frame was good.

Innes asked where he had found it. He got no information there. The shopkeeper had taken it in with a lot of other office furnishings. He was willing to sell it cheap. The frame could be fixed up.

So Innes bought it—one hopes for $75.

He said nothing until he and his wife had left the shop.

"Do you remember, Lizzie," he asked, "how mad I was because they made me paint the name on the engine?"

He kept the picture for the rest of his life and was pleased with it. Just before his death in 1894, discussing it with a reporter for the New York *Herald*, he said, "You see, I had to show the double tracks and the roundhouse, whether they were in perspective or not. But there is considerable power of painting in it and the distance is excellent."

His daughter, Mrs. Jonathan Scott Bartley, inherited the picture when he died. When it came onto the market some years later, John Walker, chief curator of the National Gallery, borrowed it and one day mentioned to Mrs. Huddleston Rogers that it was one of Innes' best works. Mrs. Rogers bought it and presented it to the museum.

How much Mrs. Rogers had to pay for the canvas is known only to herself, Mrs. Bartley, and the income-tax collector. But anyone may appraise it to suit himself. It is not for sale. It is highly prized by its present owners. It cannot be duplicated. And it is an Innes.

24 *The Hoboken Ferry*

THE Hoboken Ferry is easily the oldest unit in the Lackawanna system and, come to think about it, the oldest continuously operating unit you are likely to find on any transportation map. It is older than most of the now populous New Jersey suburban towns; older, even, than the United States.

It was chartered just before the Revolution as a means of getting to a place called Hoebuck (previously Hoboock) which, at that time, seemed a fairly long distance from New York. The first craft on the run were sailboats with oars and paddles as auxiliary power. The service got so bad in 1785 that the ferry franchise was put up at auction and sold to one Sylvanus Lawrence for £37 a year. Then Mr. Lawrence was unable to raise the £37.

There were other lessees and other sales. It is interesting to note that the rent kept going up steadily every year or so and that none of the lessees seemed to be able to meet the tariff, whatever it was.

The equipment kept changing, along with the operators. One of the most successful of the early boats was a sort of canalboat with sails, known locally as a periauger. With these fine craft and the sort of wind you could expect almost any day, Joseph Smith, the lessee, was able to drum up a considerable business in freight. His price list, established in 1799 by an aldermanic committee, still makes interesting reading.

A passenger rode for ninepence, a coach for eight shillings sixpence, a chaise or top chair for three shillings sixpence, an ordinary sedan chair for two and six, and a sleigh for three and six.

You could get a horse or a cow across for a shilling ninepence, a bushel of salt for tuppence ha'penny, a hogshead of wine or molasses for eight shillings, a mahogany chair for tuppence, as against a common chair for a penny. A bale of cotton went for two shillings, an empty hogshead for one shilling, a hundred cabbages for one and six, and shad for two shillings a hundred. The rates were deemed satisfactory to all, but nobody got rich trying to collect them, and the travel between New York and Hoboken remained something of a dubious adventure until, in 1810, John Stevens was given a lease to try a steamboat. Only a few had ever seen one, but everybody in New York knew how marvelous they were.

In 1811 the craft was finished and the ferry franchise farmed out to David Goodwin, in consideration of $1,000 a year and a free pass *in perpetuum* for Stevens and his family. The pass was still being issued to descendants of Stevens fifteen years ago.

The steamboat christened "Juliana" was undoubtedly a success. On September 23, 1811, she made sixteen trips between Vesey Street, New York, and Hoboken, carrying an average of a hundred passengers a trip.

Colonel Stevens was elated to find that his boat had doubled Robert Fulton's estimated average of "seven or eight trips in one day." After her shakedown service in 1811, she was laid up until April 12, 1812. During that summer she earned $4,308, which included $210 for the transport of a thousand head of cattle. Colonel Stevens put in some improvements at his dock, including floating stairs. He foresaw even bigger business in 1813, but he had no warning that he was not going to get any of it.

When the "Juliana" came from winter quarters in the spring, Stevens was greeted by an injunction. It seems that the New York Legislature, claiming exclusive jurisdiction over the navigable waters of the state, had given to Robert Fulton and Robert Livingston a monopoly in the operation of steamboats on rivers. They in turn had given an exclusive license to the Paulus Hook Ferry Company to use steam ferryboats from any point on the New Jersey shore for a distance three miles north of the ferry. Hoboken and Weehawken came within the three-mile limit and Colonel Stevens and the "Juliana" were ruled out of business.

He sent the ship up to Connecticut, where it was dismantled. He ran periaugers and similar scows on the old ferry route for a few years, then sold his lease to John, Robert, and Samuel Swartwouts.

In 1818 the New York Ferry Committee decided that the landing place at the foot of Murray Street was too remote from market and recommended removal of the terminal to Barclay Street, where it was to stay for quite a long time. In the same report the committee announced that the charter was once more being taken up for non-payment of rent and transferred to Philip Hone. Odd people got into the ferry business in those days, not the least remarkable being Mr. Hone. He was a social light who kept a diary, leaned toward socialism, and became mayor of New York. He was also interested in transportation, an experiment that took him up into the Pennsylvania coal fields in the days of the gravity railroads and gave his name to Honesdale.

For some reason the Stevens steam ferry seems to have been retired at the time Hone took over the Hoboken franchise. It is mentioned in the committee's report that the new lessee had promised to provide a good "horse boat in the place of the steamboat required by the lease." Horse boats were a species of paddle craft, powered by horse-operated treadmills, and their use brought a great outcry from Stevens.

Stevens had left the ferry business to open a public house in Hoboken, and the burden of his complaint was that the bar on the boat constituted unfair competition. He charged that Hone worked crippled horses and mules fifteen hours a day and made passage across the river uncomfortable, while thirsty passengers, "cabined, cribbed, and confined" on the boat, must patronize the bar or continue to thirst. The longer the voyage, he observed, the more money in Hone's purse.

There were outcries against Hone from other sources. One disgruntled but anonymous passenger published a handbill giving an account of his trip across the river:

We embarked on an aquatic conveyance called by the people of these parts a horse boat. But I am inclined to believe that this novelty is a mere sham, a trick upon travellers.

There are a dozen sorry nags in this contrivance, which go round in a circular walk with halters on one end and beams at the other extremity. How this orbicular movement can promote the rectilinear advancement of this mammoth boat is to me a mystery. And as we were six hours in crossing the river, I suspect that they go and come with the tide and that the horses are a mere catch-penny to bring their masters the trigesimose-cundal part of a dollar more on every head than the customary ferriage levied on passengers. . . .

However, despite the roars of the public and Colonel Stevens, Mr. Hone kept his lease. In September, 1819, he was granted exclusive right to operate a ferry to New Jersey from Christopher Street. And about that time Stevens began to prepare memorials to the Corporation of the City of New York and later to the New York State Legislature, protesting the monopoly. Stevens pointed out that Fulton's steamboats were hauling multitudes of passengers quickly and comfortably to Long Island points and to Staten Island. He declared that, in transferring his right, he had provided that there could be no further transfer without his knowledge and consent; that he had sold to David Goodwin and later to John, Robert, and Samuel Swartwouts; and that they in turn had sold, without his knowledge, to Philip Hone.

A suit based on this premise was compromised in May, 1821, when Hone sold his rights in the Barclay Street and Spring Street ferries to John C. and Robert L. Stevens, who then took their fight to Albany.

Colonel Stevens declared that the grant given to Fulton and Livingston was worthless, but that he was not ready to argue about it. To preserve peace and give proper service to the people of New York City and Hoboken, he said, he was willing to pay a royalty "for their grant of a right to run steamboats on the Hoboken Ferry."

The legislature declined to take up the matter. Stevens then announced that he intended to provide steam service on the Hoboken Ferry with permission or without it. He served notice of what he was going to do on the proprietors of the Paulus Hook Ferry. Then, on November 3, 1821, he incorporated the Hoboken Steamboat Ferry Company.

In April, 1822, the steamship "Hoboken," just completed, was brought to the Barclay Street terminal and exhibited to members of the New York Common Council. A contemporary newspaper account said of it:

The Steamboat "Hoboken" moves through the water at nine miles an hour. It is ninety-eight feet long on deck, twenty-six feet wide, with a draft of only three and one-half feet. The ship is of two hundred tons burden and between nine and ten feet deep in the middle of the hold. She can afford accommodations for at least a hundred persons.

The boat was placed in service on May 11, 1822, and on May 14 it drew a rave notice in the New York *Evening Post:*

The beautiful steam ferryboat built by Messrs. Stevens to ply between this city and Hoboken has commenced its trips. The construction of this boat, which unites all that is desirable in speed, convenience, safety and economy, is highly creditable to the gentlemen who planned it and, in fact, to the mechanical ingenuity of the country.

The city of New York, having decided it had the supreme right to license its own ferries "in any manner not prohibited by United States patent," gave Stevens permission to operate a line from Spring Street in July, 1823. And in September of that year the ferryboat "Pioneer" was given a trial run with members of the common council as invited guests. The boat was faster than the "Hoboken" and a little more gaudy. It had a "Ladies' Cabin" below decks with carpets on the floor, mirrors on the wall, and open fireplaces at either end. It was a great success.

Other boats came quickly: the "Fairy Queen" which displaced the last of the horse boats on the Canal Street Ferry in April, 1825; the "Newark," 1828; "Passaic," 1844; "John Fitch," 1846; "James Rumsey," 1846. The "James Rumsey" was destroyed by fire in the slip at Barclay Street in 1853, but the engines were salvaged and placed in the "Paterson" in 1854. The "James Watt," built in 1851, was destroyed by fire in 1870. The "Chancellor Livingston," built in 1853, was chartered by the government in 1861 as a transport and remained in this service a year. The second "Hoboken" was built in 1861, taken over by the government a year later, and lost in the Burnside expedition the same year. A third "Hoboken" was built and christened in 1863.

The community of Hoboken had prospered along with the ferry. There was a considerable land boom in the period immediately preceding the Civil War. The population increased rapidly, and there was a brisk local business. The place was incorporated as a city on March 28, 1855.

The opening of the Christopher Street Ferry in July, 1836, eventually caused the abandonment of the Spring Street and Canal Street ferries. Ferryboat pilots and engineers were brought under the Federal steamboat inspection service in 1853 and subjected to licensing provisions in 1864. The first night boat was put into service on the ferries in 1856.

The end of the Civil War saw the advent of bigger boats and a tendency to standardization. The "Morristown," built by John Stuart of Hoboken in 1864, was 632 gross tons, 198 feet long, with a beam of 44 feet and a draft of 12 feet. The "Hackensack," which the same builder turned out in 1871, was nearly a thousand gross tons, 215 feet wide, with a beam of 50 feet and a draft of 12.03 feet.

The "Secaucus," launched by John Stuart in 1873, represented something new in engine-room refinement and passenger comfort. The boat had a single deck and wooden hull, was 214 feet long, 46½ feet wide, with a draft of 12.6 feet and a gross tonnage of 971, and cost $121,140. It was sold to the Carteret Ferry Company in 1920.

The first steel-hulled ferryboat to see service in the river was the "Lackawanna" which was built by Ward Stanton and Company at Newburgh, New York, in 1881. She cost $76,000, was 822 gross tons and was in continuous service until 1907, when she was sold to the Norfolk and Washington Steamboat Company. She was later permanently sunk in the Potomac River.

Edwin L. Brady of New York got a patent on a screw-propelled ferryboat in 1867 and built two 900-ton ships. That they were ever used as ferryboats is problematical, and they ended their days as dredges in the mouth of the Mississippi.

Then, in 1879, a double-ended ferryboat with twin screws at either end was given a considerable test on the Mersey River between Liverpool and Birkenhead, England. It set a style in hull construction that was to last for many years. The "Montclair" and "Orange," constructed in 1886, were the last side-wheel vessels built for the ferry service. The "Bergen," launched in October, 1888, was the first of the screw-driven ships, and an outstanding novelty.

The "Bergen" was a single-decked, steel boat, 203 feet long and 62 feet wide, with a draft of 10 feet. It was powered by a triple expansion engine coupled to a line shaft that ran the entire length of the hull, with a screw at each end. In operation one screw pulled and the other one pushed. The design was a collaboration to which numerous engineers contributed. The propellers were four blades, 8 feet in diameter and 9½-foot pitch. Lighting was by Pintsch gas. The cost of the boat was $135,835.

After a series of comparative tests with the "Orange," the most recent paddle-wheel boat, Mr. Stevens announced:

"In point of handling, the 'Bergen' compares favorably with any ferryboat on the river. . . .

"She can stop in a shorter distance notwithstanding her higher speed.

"Practically, the 'Bergen' is preferred by passengers and pilots alike. While the boat is by no means perfect, she is the best boat we have . . . and will furnish a type for our future boats. . . ."

Except for the double-decked superstructure that came in with the "Hamburg" in 1891, the ferryboat from then on was much as we know it today.

Roswell Eldridge and Lewis A. Eldridge, who had been running the Astoria Ferry and the Long Island Railroad Ferry, took over the Fourteenth Street Ferry on January 1, 1896, and a year later bought the lower ferries of the Hoboken Ferry Company. These lines had been in the Stevens family seventy-five years. The Eldridges operated until the end of 1904. In a lease dated December 29 of that year, the Delaware, Lackawanna and Western Railroad assumed the management of the Hoboken Ferry Company and made it a part of the Lackawanna system.

There was no fuss about the arrangement. The only difference apparent was that pilots were paid more money, ticket choppers were installed in the sales department, and faster boats were built for the Barclay Street route. The "Scranton," built in 1904, was 1,462 gross tons, 230 feet long, 62½ feet wide, drew 16 feet and cost $211,478. The "Elmira," a similar ship, was delivered in 1905. The "Binghamton" and "Scandinavia," boats of the same size and pattern, were put into service the same year. William H. Truesdale was president of the railroad; T. W. Lee, general passenger agent; L. Bush, chief engineer; and P. J. Flynn, freight traffic manager. On March 1, 1905, John M. Emery was appointed superintendent of the ferry department and Benjamin Schoppe, chief engineer.

There was a fire on August 7, 1905, that destroyed the Hoboken Ferry terminal and made ashes out of the Lackawanna depot. The ferryboat "Hopatcong," in which the blaze started, was towed to Weehawken Flats and left there, a complete loss. No one was hurt, and, except for the few hours required to clear away debris at the railroad terminal, neither ferry nor train traffic was greatly interrupted.

A new "Lackawanna" and a new "Hopatcong," double-decked, steel-hulled boats, built for the Norfolk and Washington Steamboat Company in 1905 as the "Woodbury" and the "Callahan," were added to the Hoboken fleet in 1907, a few days before the opening of the new Hoboken terminal. The "Hoboken," fourth of the name, was launched with the "Buffalo" in 1922. These ships cost $355,399 apiece, a new record for such vessels, even on the Hudson River.

The opening of the Holland Vehicle Tunnel on November 12, 1927, caused an immediate drop of from 30 to 40 per cent on the haul of the Lackawanna ferries. By 1930 it was nearly back to normal, except for Sundays.

A reconstruction program costing $1,500,000 was started in 1930 and completed in 1935. During this period new boilers were installed in the ferryboats "Bergen," "Binghamton," "Chatham," "Elmira," "Ithaca," "Maplewood," "Montclair," "Netherlands," "Orange," "Scandinavia," and "Scranton." In addition, extensive repairs were made to the boats. Sprinkler systems were installed in all gangways. These are manually operated, so that, in the event that a vehicle catches fire, the ferryboat's engineer can immediately start the boat's fire pump and throw a curtain of water over the entire gangway.

Several of the ferryboats were originally named after steamship companies that had their terminals in the city of Hoboken. In 1935 it was decided to rename these boats, following a practice inaugurated several years before, after towns and cities along the Lackawanna system. The "Scandinavia" was changed to the "Pocono" and the "Netherlands" to the "Oswego."

The ferry racks and bridges were next to receive the attention of the management, and in March, 1936, two new racks and clusters were built between slips Nos. 4 and 5, Hoboken Terminal, replacing old racks, followed by two new ferry racks between slips Nos. 2 and 4 at Hoboken. This was the first time Greenheart piling was used, brought here from South America. New racks were also constructed at Fourteenth Street, Hoboken, in December, 1940, followed by considerable repairs to the racks at Christopher Street, New York, in March, 1941.

Bulkheads, both longitudinal and athwartship, were built into the ferryboats when constructed, the longitudinal bulkheads forming an inner skin, so that the hold would not be flooded, even though the outer shell of the boat was punctured. The athwartship bulkheads afford still further protection in that, should water find its way into the interior of the boat, it could be localized in one single compartment or section. In order to have access to the various compartments, manually operated watertight doors have been installed in the athwartship bulkheads.

In 1939 emergency lighting systems which operate from storage batteries were installed in the boats. This lighting system is always available for use as a substitute for the boat's regular system, should the necessity arise. Because of the many requests received from business concerns and trucking associations, a special ferry service was started on Monday, April 4, 1938, for vehicles carrying commodities which could not lawfully be transported on ferryboats carrying passengers. As the Port Authority regulations prohibited the transportation of many of these commodities through their tunnels, it was necessary, prior to the inauguration of this service, for truck operators to route their vehicles over the George Washington Bridge in order to reach points in New York City.

After this country entered the Second World War, government authorities wanted to increase the facilities for ship-repair work in the large plants located in Hoboken, New Jersey, and accordingly the U.S. Navy acquired possession of the property owned by the ferry company at the foot of Fourteenth Street, Hoboken, in order to convert the ferry terminal into a ship-repair yard. This made it necessary to discontinue the ferry operating between Fourteenth Street, Hoboken, and West Twenty-third Street, New York, New York, in April, 1942.

Upon the discontinuance of the Fourteenth Street Ferry Lines, the two single-deck ferryboats, "Hoboken" and "Buffalo," which can accommodate a larger number of vehicles than any of the company's other ferryboats, were transferred to the Christopher Street route. This discontinuance left the company with surplus boats on their hands and the ferryboat "Orange" was taken out of service on February 1, 1942, and the "Montclair" and "Maplewood" on April 28 of that year. The "Orange" and "Montclair," both side-wheel ferryboats, were sold on March 2, 1944, to the Maritime Salvage Corporation of North Bergen, New Jersey, and the "Maplewood," on June 22, 1946, to the Tampa–New Orleans Tampico Air Lines, Inc., of New York, New York.

On August 11, 1946, fire, starting on the pier at the Brighton Marine Repair Yard, West New Brighton, Staten Island, spread to the ferryboat "Ithaca." Being hauled on dry dock, the boat could not be removed, the result being that the entire superstructure was destroyed and the boat put out of service.

Because of continued loss of traffic, both vehicular and passenger, it became evident in the year 1945 that there was no necessity for three ferry lines to New York City. After intensive study, the management decided that the Twenty-third Street route would be the logical one to abandon. On December 9, 1946, the Interstate Commerce Commission authorized the change, and the service was discontinued as of December 31, 1946.

Since the early part of the century the Pennsylvania Railroad System, the Central Railroad Company of New Jersey, the Erie Railroad, and the Delaware, Lackawanna and Western Railroad Company all had operated ferry lines to West Twenty-third Street, New York. In addition to these railroad ferries, the Electric Ferries also operated a ferry line between West Twenty-third Street, New York, and Weehawken, New Jersey. The various railroads discontinued their ferry service at West Twenty-third Street on the following dates:

Pennsylvania Railroad—November 30, 1910
Central Railroad Company of New Jersey—November 14, 1941
Erie Railroad Company—July 5, 1942
Delaware, Lackawanna and Western Railroad Company
   (Fourteenth Street Line)—April 26, 1942
Delaware, Lackawanna and Western Railroad Company
   (to downtown Hoboken)—December 31, 1946
Electric Ferries—July 31, 1943

25 G. Washington Slept Here

THIRTY-five thousand working people ride the Lackawanna trains and ferries from the New Jersey suburbs into New York every morning. The same 35,000 toilers travel back at night, a process which for the goodly part of a century has been taken as a matter of course. The figure does not include thousands of shoppers and pleasure seekers. Most of northern Jersey has been transformed by quick transportation into an economic part of the great metropolis. Thus much of New York is not really a part of New York at all.

Many of the 35,000 detached New Yorkers come from as far away as Dover, 39 miles northwest of Hoboken, or from Gladstone, which is about the same distance straight west. A few make the daily run from Lake Hopatcong. There are some who make regular trips between New York and Blairstown, or even Stroudsburg, although, admittedly, one could hardly class Stroudsburg as one of Manhattan's more convenient environs.

Not a few of these communities along the Lackawanna right-of-way are of considerable antiquity and historic interest. Hoboock or Hoebuck, or Hoboken, is one of them. It seems to have been looked upon with interest by Hendrik Hudson from the deck of the "Half Moon"; and there was a settlement on Hoboken Point before the Revolutionary War. Morristown, which provided headquarters for George Washington in 1777, is another town that was well established when most of New Jersey was unsettled land. Clifton, Bernardsville, Maplewood, Orange, Passaic, Oxford, and Madison were also doing a considerable business before the uprising of the colonies. The places where Washington slept are so numerous in the neighborhood that nobody bothers to mention them.

Like other towns on the Lackawanna map, the pioneer towns of New Jersey sprang up along the trails that led from the hardships of known valleys to the mysteries of the unknown. The trails had been made originally by animals instinctively taking the easiest routes between food and water; they were enlarged by Indian trackers on the same quest and further beaten into the soil by white woodsmen. What traffic there was from civilization to and from the wilderness naturally followed these dim lanes. Inns and taverns came to cater to the trappers and traders, and little settlements grew up alongside the inns. So it had been before in man's migrations, and so it was to be again.

The whole region, from the Delaware to the Hudson, is thickly overlaid with tradition. The pleasing legends evolved around stone fireplaces in the taverns of the Jersey back country two hundred years ago lose none of their attractiveness in combination with the new folklore that the railroad brought. New tradition was faithful to the pattern of the old. It is difficult to believe that some of these towns, with an atmosphere more old-worldly than that of Stratford-on-Avon, are more recent than, say, Buffalo or Chicago. But the old surveys do not lie. Many of the Lackawanna's suburban communities owe their existence to the Lackawanna itself. What one fails to recollect is that the railroad has been hauling people around New Jersey for a hundred years, which, as time is reckoned in America, adds up to a considerable antiquity.

There is a story whose origins escape us, about a New York financier who used to ride into New York in the early days of the Morris and Essex. It was his custom, so the record reads, to stand in the middle aisle of the coach to avoid "snake-heads," the strap rails, which had a way of coming loose and curling up through the floor. To many commuters, riding in safety and comfort at something like sixty miles an hour, that may sound like a bit of fantasy almost as old as the legends of George Washington's winter at Morristown.

There are plenty of residents alive in Summit today who remember when Summit was really a summit that wet weather rendered all but inaccessible—the days when an arriving traveler was asked, "Did you come in with 'Moses Taylor' or 'George Miller' or 'Joshua Williams'?" Nobody talked about the "five-fifteen" or the "six-o-three," because time was one of the great intangibles of railroading. Instead, trains were called by the names of the locomotives that hauled them. "Did you come in with 'John I. Blair'?" was the equivalent between 1860 and 1890 of the query, "Did you cross on the 'Queen Mary' or the 'Ile de France'?"

The children of Summit in a somewhat latter day used to congregate around the railroad station of a Sunday afternoon to sit on the rails and make noises like whistles. Because it was expressly forbidden, they had always wanted to play on the railroad tracks. And on Sunday they got the opportunity, because the trains did not run.

A few of these children, now well along in years, recall that most of the early-morning commuters were men—earnest characters who wore beards and carried canes. They never relaxed. They seldom smiled. The journey to Hoboken, apparently, was too serious an undertaking to permit of levity. Today the commuter is clean-shaven and carries a brief case. He reads the comic strips as he romps along to the countinghouse or the brokerage office or the dry-goods store in the big city, and the old days seem far in the past.

The idea of commuting had become so firmly established in 1930 that the electrification of the northern New Jersey suburban lines can hardly be given credit for starting it. But there is not much doubt about the effect of fast and continuous service on the numerous towns where George Washington once slept. It made possible real-estate developments and housing projects more miles from Broadway than could ever have been thought about before. And it gave an opportunity to men of moderate means, as well as millionaires, to live in the country. Today there is probably no more attractive suburban area in the United States. The towns that stretch in pleasant succession through a region of mountains and lakes are new and fresh looking and all of them brightly prosperous. With frequent, fast train service, the farthest of them is no farther from Manhattan than Bloomfield was fifty years ago.

The main line of electrification runs from Hoboken to Dover, via Newark and Summit, with branches from Newark to Montclair and from Summit to Gladstone. There is steam service from Hoboken to Dover, via Passaic, Paterson, and Boonton. This route traverses some of the most popular resort country in the East.

One of the earliest and most popular of the Lackawanna suburban communities is the Orange-Maplewood group: Orange, East Orange, West Orange, South Orange, and Maplewood. The components are individual municipalities, but together they make up a band of homogeneous population that lies along the right-of-way from 11 miles to 16 miles west of Hoboken. The towns, which rise in a series of terraces from the Newark meadows toward the summit of the rugged Watchung Mountain Range, are the heritors of a community that existed here long before the Revolution. Even in stagecoach days the beauty of the area and its better climate had made it a haunt of New Yorkers trying to get away from it all. If George Washington slept here, it was not entirely on account of the British.

Modern development of the communities has been carried out with care and intelligence. It is possible to drive for a whole afternoon over broad roads through natural parks which seem to be almost as primitive as they were in 1678, when the first settlers called it Mountain Plantations, and still never get out of the combined corporate limits of the suburbs. Then one may stand on Eagle Rock, principal feature of a 408-acre park, and look eastward across the homes of 10,000,000 people. To the west, virgin forest carries on to the horizon.

The Oranges and Maplewood support thirty-six public grammar schools, nine parochial schools, four high schools, six junior high schools, two colleges, four private academies, ninety-two churches, four parks, twenty-two playgrounds, two golf courses, a public stadium, eleven theaters, and more than 150 clubs. The population at the last census was 166,000. Unofficial estimates put the present figure at more than a quarter million.

The community is proud of its Art Center and the percentage of its inhabitants whose names are in *Who's Who*. The place where Washington slept in this neighborhood is the Timothy Ball House in Maplewood. A plaque on a walnut tree outside the house mentions that G. Washington used to tie his horse to it.

West of Maplewood is Millburn, a thriving town whose position near the mountainside gives it great beauty. Millburn was settled fifty years before the Revolution by Dutch farmers from Elizabeth and Montclair. The early town prospered with paper mills and hat factories that are long since gone. The plant of one of them, the 150-year-old Diamond Paper Mill, was transformed by the Newark Art Theater Guild into the Paper Mill Theater, which is the center of the town's cultural life.

Springfield, a mile from the Lackawanna station, is one place in the locality which has no record of Washington's having stayed long enough to sleep. There was a bitter fight for the place on June 23, 1780, most of it in the main street. During the battle the Continentals ran out of gun wadding, and the British had begun to move in when the Reverend James Caldwell, of Millburn, broke open the church and got an armful of Watts hymnbooks. Tossing them to the revolutionaries, he is said to have shouted "Give 'em Watts, boys! Give 'em Watts what!" The quotation is given with some variants, but, anyway, it was a pretty thought.

Short Hills, a half mile farther west, is the home of much wealth and three golf clubs.

Summit, 20 miles from Broadway, on the crest of a ridge in beautiful hill country, was laid out in the midst of a dense woods. Its temperate summer climate has made it a mecca for people from coastal towns as far away as Boston, but it is still a New York suburb.

Chatham, the next station northwest of Summit, has a colonial history and character. Two centuries have not obliterated the marks of its origins or made much change in G. Washington's billets. Day's Tavern, a two-and-one-half-story frame structure just east of the business district, was much frequented by Washington and his officers and is still in business. The Elm Tree Inn, which has been referred to as "The New Tavern," is also fairly well preserved. It is on the western edge of town and looks much as it did when it was built in 1811.

Six miles farther along the line, on the outskirts of Madison, is the Bottle Hill Tavern, once a post house for the Elizabeth-Morristown stage line. There is no record that David Brant, the proprietor, ever rented a room to G. Washington. The representative of the high brass who slept here was the Marquis de Lafayette.

Madison's suburban modernity rests lightly on its rich historical background. It has a million-dollar municipal building, gift of Mrs. Marcellus Hartley Dodge, niece of the late John D. Rockefeller. One of its prize exhibits is the Sayre House, headquarters of Mad Anthony Wayne in 1745. Drew University, on its western outskirts, keeps green the memory of Daniel Drew.

Many of Madison's residents are descendants of the founding families, and the ancient traditions have been well preserved. The town, as a place to live, is one of the most charming on the Lackawanna. Like its neighbors, it is a place of surprising natural beauty.

Morristown, 30 miles from Hoboken, is the gateway to Morristown National Historical Park. Its homes and living accommodations are among the finest in New Jersey. Much of colonial America lives here, its preservation assured since the day when the Continental Army marched in and established it as a strategic base to confine the British to the vicinity of New York. And, of course, G. Washington slept here. Not only that, he starved here—and his army with him—for days at a time on rations that made the parched corn of Valley Forge seem like a continuous banquet. He maintained his headquarters at Ford House, which has been preserved. Ford House ranks second only to Mount Vernon as a storehouse of Washington relics.

There are other shrines of Revolutionary legend: Jockey Hollow, where the bulk of the colonial army had a base camp from 1779 to 1781; Fort Nonsense, an earthen redoubt which got its present name after its original purpose had been forgotten; the Historical Museum which contains many of Washington's letters, a Gilbert Stuart portrait, and many of the general's personal effects; the Wick House, home of one of Washington's cavalry captains and his daughter Tempe, who hid her horse in her bedroom to save it from confiscation by the military.

Just outside of Morristown on the way north is Magnetic Hill, providing an optical illusion which, fortunately, is not noticeable when studied from a train window. Motorists come from miles around to investigate what has been advertised as a suspension of gravity. You stop your car on a down slope, and immediately it seems to roll backwards, under no power, up hill.

Two or three miles farther on, just north of the Whippany River Bridge, is the Alfred Vail House, a barnlike building where, in the

fall of 1837, Samuel F. B. Morse and Alfred Vail developed the telegraph. On a January day in 1838, over three miles of wire looped
about this building, Vail rapped out the first recorded message in
the Morse code. He observed, somewhat hopefully, "A patient
waiter is no loser." Nearby is the site of the Speedwell Iron Works
where Stephen Vail, Albert's father, supervised the machining of
the shaft for the "Savannah," the first vessel to cross the Atlantic
under auxiliary steam power.

Morris Plains is an unobtrusive residential community. Beyond it,
to the north, is Mount Tabor, a summer resort to which electrification has brought a year-round existence. A few miles farther on is
Denville, with a similar history. Denville at any time of the year is
busy enough to look like a larger town. In the summer season, when
city dwellers come in to play among its nine lakes, its population
will add up to a possible fifteen thousand.

Dover, the end of the main-line electrification project, is socially
and industrially one of the most progressive of New Jersey's towns.
Once called "the Pittsburgh of Jersey," it was a thriving port on the
Morris Canal and is still an important distribution point for iron
ore from a considerable neighboring district.

Active civic organizations and an altitude of 700 feet, not to
mention a location close to the lake district, have given the place
new popularity as a suburb. That it is almost as close to Stroudsburg
as to Hoboken makes this new phase of Dover's odd existence the
more remarkable.

Mountain Lakes, two miles west of Boonton, on the Boonton
branch, has the physical possibilities of another Venice and a railroad
station serving about a dozen lakes. Begun as a frank real-estate development, it caught the fancy of about as many home-seekers as
fishermen and now has a growing population of commuters.

Boonton, to the east on the steam line, is 30 miles from the ferry
slip, and is likewise a combination of home and summer resort and
fishing and hunting preserve. While its local businessmen might
object to its being labeled a suburb, it undoubtedly is just that to
many people. Sometimes called "the City on the Hill," it clings to
a ledge overlooking Rockaway Gorge and somehow resembles a
New England manufacturing center. Founded as an industrial town
in the eighties, it retains this character, no matter what may be the

interests of the people who live in its spacious residence districts. Bakelite was first manufactured here by Richard W. Seabury in an old rubber plant. At this writing the industrial district includes two nationally known hosiery mills, a gunpowder factory, dynamite and torpedo plants. Cheap water power, low taxes, a healthful climate, and magnificent mountain scenery are Boonton's chief assets. At a short distance are sections known as Rockaway Valley, Parsippany, Troy Hills, Lake Hiawatha, Fayson Lakes—regions of great beauty where lush farmlands alternate with lakes and hunting grounds and dark forests.

Paterson, through which the steam trains pass on their way from the lake districts to New York, has a population of something over 150,000 (estimated) and has never been a suburb of anything since Alexander Hamilton, Secretary of the Treasury, helped to found it in 1791.

Hamilton gave his blessing to the Society for Establishing Useful Manufactures, which he thought might be interested in the falls of the Passaic. The New Jersey Legislature voted the company perpetual exemption from county and township taxes, and gave it the right to hold property, improve rivers, build canals, and raise $100,000 by lottery. The company then accepted a grant of 700 acres at the falls and went into business with Major Pierre L'Enfant, designer of Washington, D.C., in charge of building the raceways. The new community was named for Governor Paterson. It has long been one of the country's leading producers of fine textiles.

Passaic, 11 miles from Hoboken, is one of the district's oldest communities. It was founded in 1678 by Hartman Michielsen, who bought Menehenicke Island, now Pulaski Park, from the Leni-Lenape Indians for a trading post. Other Dutch adventurers followed him. The British occupied the settlement during the Revolution. When they left, Passaic became a river port of some consequence, distributing farm produce. Dutch, Irish, and German families made up the population when the railroads came. They were followed by Slavic immigrants in the seventies. George B. Waterhouse started a woolen manufacturing plant in that period. In 1890 the Botany Woolen Mills were opened up, and Passaic has since taken a leading place in the country's wool trade.

Lyndhurst, less than ten miles from New York, is a growing com-

mercial and residential community. It is an older place than you
might think and was founded by some promoter from Barbados,
whose name unfortunately has been lost. It was first called New
Barbados Neck but later changed its name in honor of Lord Lyndhurst, a frequent visitor. William R. Travers, a wealthy New Yorker,
laid out a large block of Lyndhurst's houses along the Passaic in
1880 and built a summer home, where he entertained August Belmont and "Boss" Tweed.

You get back to the G. Washington influence when you follow
the branch of the electric line that turns off to the north at Newark
for Montclair. Three miles from the junction is Bloomfield, with a
population which the new census may show to be something more
than fifty thousand. It is an old settlement that has suddenly found
itself a modern residential and industrial extension of Newark. The
founding fathers back in antiquity called the place Wardesson,
which is Leni-Lenape for "crooked place," but a more modern
population rechristened it in 1796 to honor Joseph Bloomfield,
Revolutionary general and governor of New Jersey. Its original
tract of 20 square miles has been cut up to make the towns of
Montclair, Belleville, Glen Ridge, and Nutley.

There is a story that George Washington, presumably looking
for a place to sleep, came to visit the home of Caleb Davis in Bloomfield during the Revolutionary War, found Benedict Arnold already
present, and moved on. It does not sound likely. Arnold may not
have been a likeable chap, but he was an officer in good standing
until the capture of Major André, and after that he was not visiting
anybody in Bloomfield.

Glen Ridge, the next station north, is a commuters' town with
a highly developed civic consciousness. It has a municipal government with a mayor and council, but its affairs are really run by its
Woman's Club, Men's Forum, Home and School Association, and
Civic Conference Committee, which fix up the slate for the dollar-
a-year council and school board. It has a three-block business
district, carefully planned, and a residence area with winding shady
streets. It is free from apartments, billboards, telephone poles, and
overhead wires.

Montclair, at the end of the line, broke with Bloomfield in 1868,
when the parent town opposed the construction of a railroad from

Jersey City to the New York state line. The township's history began in 1666, when Philip Carteret offered inducements to settlers to establish a town on the Passaic River. The Montclair end of it was originally an outlying residence district, to which gravitated much wealth from New York. The present town is the wealthiest per capita in the state and second in the nation.

The second branch of the electric line, which turns south from Summit, goes through New Providence on the second slope of the Watchung Mountains. Strictly zoned, New Providence has grown quietly and unobtrusively. It is a pleasant, dignified town, completely in step with the other modern developments in Lackawanna suburbs. Once this delightful spot was called Turkey. The name was changed to New Providence after a church balcony fell down without hurting anybody.

Murray Hill, to the south, is the home of the Bell Laboratory's project. Stirling, south and west, is a community of small homes on grounds large enough for the private raising of flowers, vegetables, chickens, and dairying. The National Shrine of St. Joseph is located there. From the grounds of the shrine one may see 20 miles of the Watchung Mountains, a view that attracts thousands of visitors each year. Millington, bounded on three sides by the Passaic, is a community with resort advantages, a variety of homes and accommodations for visitors, good schools, and an exceptional public library.

Basking Ridge is described by the guidebook writers as "one of the most picturesque sections of New Jersey." Apparently the eighteenth-century settlers thought that, too. They gave the place its name after watching the animals come up from the lowlands to bask in the sun. Basking Ridge apparently had an attraction for General Charles Lee, second-in-command to Washington. Lee, ordered to rejoin the main body of the Continental Army two miles away, turned instead to pleasant dalliance in White's Tavern. He was still there when the British came in and captured him. There is a historic log church in the village, built by the Presbyterians in 1717. Near it is an oak tree, said to be five hundred years old, under which Washington once ate a picnic lunch.

Bernardsville, beyond Basking Ridge, is in the Somerset Hills, surrounded by golf clubs, tennis clubs, and baronial estates. A village of one-story frame and brick buildings at the foot of Mine Mountain, it looks like a moving-picture set, except for the schools and athletic fields that range on broad acres behind it.

A few miles farther on a winding right-of-way Far Hills and Bedminster share the same station. Beyond lies Peapack, with access to Peapack Lake, and Gladstone, the end of the line.

There are few places like this territory left in the United States, or, for that matter, anywhere in the world. The region is given over almost entirely to extensive estates, although there are several restricted residential districts for smaller homes. Besides Peapack Lake, the Raritan River, Leamington River, Legion Park Lake, and Ravine Lake contribute to the scenic loveliness of the district through which spread the Somerset Hills. Sport in this area is something on a grand scale—polo, steeple-chasing, riding to the hounds—with broad acres to play in, miles of hills to ride over. Fabulous fortunes went into the building of these great estates. Genius went into their design. And the commuters of another generation will talk of them as they do today of the Ford House or the Wick House or the Caleb Davis House, and probably debate whether or not George Washington slept here.

APPENDIX

Presidents of The Delaware, Lackawanna and Western Railroad Company and Its Antecedents

John J. Phelps *	Jan., 1850–May, 1851
John J. Phelps †	May, 1851–Feb., 1853
George D. Phelps †	Feb., 1853–Apr., 1853
George W. Scranton ‡	Dec., 1850–Apr., 1853
George D. Phelps §	Apr., 1853–Sept., 1856
Drake Mills §	Feb., 1857–Jan., 1858
Christopher R. Robert §	Jan., 1858–June, 1863
John Brisbin §	July, 1863–Aug., 1867
Samuel Sloan §	Aug., 1867–Mar., 1899
William H. Truesdale §	Mar., 1899–July, 1925
John M. Davis §	July, 1925–Jan., 1941
Wm. White §	Jan., 1941

Note: Ligett's Gap Railroad Company—name changed to The Lackawanna and Western Railroad Company, April, 1851. The Delaware and Cobb's Gap Railroad Company merged into The Lackawanna and Western Railroad Company, March, 1853; became The Delaware, Lackawanna and Western Railroad Company.

* Ligett's Gap Railroad Company
† The Lackawanna and Western Railroad Company
‡ The Delaware and Cobb's Gap Railroad Company
§ The Delaware, Lackawanna and Western Railroad Company

Managers (Directors)

January, 1850 to December 31, 1950

John I. Blair *†‡	Jan., 1850–Dec., 1899
Andrew Bedford *	Jan., 1850–Mar., 1850
Jeremiah Clark *	Jan., 1850–Mar., 1850
Henry W. Drinker *	Jan., 1850–Mar., 1850
William E. Dodge *†‡	Mar., 1850–May, 1858
	Jan., 1860–Feb., 1883
Charles Fuller *	Jan., 1850–Mar., 1850
Frederick R. Griffen *†	Jan., 1850–May, 1852
Daniel S. Miller *†‡	Jan., 1850–Dec., 1853
Joseph C. Platt *	Jan., 1850–Mar., 1850
Joseph H. Scranton *‡	Jan., 1850–Mar., 1850
	Feb., 1867–June, 1872
George W. Scranton *†‡	Jan., 1850–Mar., 1861
George Bulkley *†‡	Dec., 1850–Apr., 1882
Henry Hotchkiss *†‡	Mar., 1850–Dec., 1853
John Howland *†‡	Mar., 1850–Dec., 1853
Edward Mowry *†	Mar., 1850–Dec., 1851
Drake Mills *†‡	Mar., 1850–Feb., 1857
	Feb., 1858–Feb., 1863
Josiah B. Williams *†‡	Mar., 1850–Dec., 1853
George D. Phelps †	Jan., 1853–Feb., 1853
John J. Phelps †‡	Feb., 1853–Dec., 1865
John Bradley ‡	Jan., 1854–Jan., 1855
Roswell Sprague ‡	Jan., 1854–Feb., 1857
Moses Taylor ‡	Jan., 1854–May, 1882
Thomas Tileston ‡	Jan., 1854–Apr., 1854

* Ligett's Gap Railroad Company
† The Lackawanna and Western Railroad Company
‡ The Delaware, Lackawanna and Western Railroad Company

Samuel Willets *	Jan., 1855–Jan., 1858
Henry Young	Jan., 1855–Feb., 1868
Rufus R. Graves	Jan., 1856–Aug., 1876
Thomas McElrath	Jan., 1856–Jan., 1858
Samuel L. Mitchell	Jan., 1856–Dec., 1863
William E. Warren	Jan., 1856–Jan., 1858
Howell L. Williams	Jan., 1857–Jan., 1858
Christopher R. Robert	Jan., 1857–Jan., 1857
	Jan., 1858–Jan., 1859
David S. Dodge	May, 1858–Jan., 1860
David Hoadley	Jan., 1858–Jan., 1858
Charles H. Marshall	Jan., 1858–Sept., 1865
Robert L. Stuart	Jan., 1858–Jan., 1858
Simeon B. Chittenden	Jan., 1859–Jan., 1881
Lowell Holbrook	Jan., 1859–Feb., 1870
Samuel Wetmore	Jan., 1859–Jan., 1867
David Thompson	Feb., 1862–Feb., 1865
George M. Hollenbeck	Feb., 1863–Feb., 1865
Samuel Sloan	Feb., 1864–Aug., 1867
	Feb., 1869–Feb., 1869
	Feb., 1900–Sept., 1907
George Bliss	Feb., 1865–Feb., 1896
Percy R. Pyne	Feb., 1865–Feb., 1895
Edward Minturn	Sept., 1865–Jan., 1867
William Walter Phelps	Dec., 1865–Feb., 1886
John C. Phelps	Feb., 1867–Feb., 1870
John Brisbin	Aug., 1867–Feb., 1880
James Blair	Feb., 1868–Feb., 1878
Denning Duer	Feb., 1870–Feb., 1874
Wilson G. Hunt	Feb., 1870–Dec., 1892
Henry A. Kent	Jan., 1873–Feb., 1875
Alfred L. Dennis	Feb., 1874–Feb., 1881
Marcellus Massey	Feb., 1875–Feb., 1878
Benjamin G. Clarke	Jan., 1877–Feb., 1879
	Feb., 1880–Aug., 1892
E. W. Holbrook	Feb., 1878–Feb., 1884
William Ryle	Feb., 1878–Feb., 1881
Elias S. Higgins	Feb., 1879–Aug., 1889
Jay Gould	Feb., 1881–Feb., 1888

* This and all subsequent names are of managers of The Delaware, Lackawanna and Western Railroad Company

Russell Sage	Feb., 1881–Feb., 1891
Sidney Dillon	Feb., 1881–Feb., 1892
Edgar S. Auchincloss	Feb., 1883–Mar., 1892
William E. Dodge, Jr.	Feb., 1883–Feb., 1883
Andrew T. McClintock	Feb., 1883–Jan., 1892
Gardner R. Colby	Feb., 1884–July, 1889
Abram R. Van Nest	Feb., 1884–Feb., 1885
William H. Appleton	Feb., 1885–Feb., 1894
William W. Astor	Feb., 1887–Feb., 1905
Henry A. C. Taylor	Feb., 1889–May, 1921
Eugene Higgins	Oct., 1889–Apr., 1911
William Rockefeller	Feb., 1890–Dec., 1921
George F. Baker	Feb., 1892–Dec., 1921
Andrew H. McClintock	Feb., 1892–Feb., 1894
J. Rogers Maxwell	July, 1892–Dec., 1910
Robert F. Ballantine	Oct., 1892–Feb., 1894
James Stillman	Oct., 1892–Sept., 1914
Alexander T. Van Nest	Jan., 1893–Aug., 1896
Harris C. Fahnestock	Feb., 1894–June, 1914
Hamilton McK. Twombley	Feb., 1894–Jan., 1910
Frank Work	Feb., 1894–Mar., 1911
Frederick W. Vanderbilt	Feb., 1895–Feb., 1916
M. Taylor Pyne	Feb., 1896–Apr., 1921
Roswell G. Rolston	Feb., 1897–Aug., 1898
John D. Rockefeller, Jr.	Oct., 1898–Jan., 1915
Henry Graves	Feb., 1906–Aug., 1906
William H. Moore	Feb., 1907–Jan., 1923
William Fahnestock	Feb., 1908–June, 1936
George F. Baker, Jr.	Jan., 1910–June, 1931
William H. Truesdale	Dec., 1910–Feb., 1928
John F. Talmage	May, 1911–Feb., 1934
Stephen S. Palmer	May, 1911–Jan., 1913
Harold S. Vanderbilt	Feb., 1913–Dec., 1921
Henry R. Taylor	Nov., 1914–Dec., 1925
M. Hartley Dodge	Dec., 1914–
Edward E. Loomis	Nov., 1914–Nov., 1914
	Feb., 1916–Mar., 1917
Beekman Winthrop	Feb., 1915–Nov., 1940
William S. Jenney	Apr., 1917–Jan., 1939
Roy C. Gasser	Feb., 1922–
Percy R. Pyne	Feb., 1922–Aug., 1929

Frank Rysavy	Feb., 1922–Dec., 1923
	Feb., 1924–Feb., 1926
Samuel Sloan	Feb., 1922–Nov., 1939
Henry B. Spencer	Feb., 1922–Feb., 1926
Paul Moore	Feb., 1923–
Jackson E. Reynolds	Dec., 1923–Jan., 1924
Clarence M. Woolley	Feb., 1926–Feb., 1941
Lowell R. Burch	Feb., 1926–Nov., 1936
Horace Havemeyer	Feb., 1926–Mar., 1933
David F. Houston	Feb., 1928–July, 1935
Roy E. Tomlinson	Feb., 1930–
Henry S. Sturgis	June, 1931–Oct., 1941
John M. Davis	Apr., 1933–Mar., 1944
Arthur G. Hoffman	Feb., 1934–Feb., 1947
Arthur A. Houghton, Jr.	Sept., 1935
Carl P. Dennett	Feb., 1937–Nov., 1943
John G. Enderlin	Feb., 1937–Apr., 1941
	May, 1944–Dec., 1945
	Feb., 1946–Nov., 1948
Willard F. Place	Feb., 1939–
Robert W. Lea	Feb., 1940–
Wm. White	Nov., 1940–
Robert Winthrop	Feb., 1941–Oct., 1943
Henry M. Reed	Apr., 1941–Aug., 1947
Robert G. Fuller	Nov., 1941–
Lewis G. Harriman	Dec., 1943–
Douglas Swift	May, 1944–Feb., 1946
Lee P. Stack	Dec., 1945–
Ralph D. Jennison	May, 1947–
William H. Moore	Sept., 1947–
W. Paul Stillman	Nov., 1948–

INDEX

A

"Abington" (engine), 65
Abington Center, 37, 39, 61, 66
Abington Wilderness, 14
Albany and Susquehanna Railroad, 92
Albro, Zeno, 31, 41, 42
American Railroad Journal, 76
Analomink River, 70
Andover, 140
André, Major, 206
Archbald, James, 88, 131, 135
Ark Swamp, 66
Armstrong, Edward, 30, 31
Armstrong Cut, 140
Army Service Forces Unit, 164
Arnold, Benedict, 206
Atlantic and Great Western Railroad, 85

B

Baker, George F., 101
Baldwin, Isaac, 72
Baldwinsville, 164
Baltimore, Lord Cecilius, 5, 6
Baltimore, Lord George, 5
Baltimore and Ohio Railroad, 63, 99, 100, 107, 155, 175
Bank of the United States, 45
Bartley, Mrs. Jonathan S., 187
Basking Bridge, 207
Beaver River, 32
Bedford, Dr. Andrew, 37, 38, 39, 40, 61, 63
Bedminster, 208
Beech, Maj. Ephraim, 70, 72, 74

Belleville, 206
Belmont, August, 206
Belvidere, 34, 55, 82, 83
Belvidere and Delaware Railroad, 71
"Bergen" (ferryboat), 193, 194, 195
Bergen Hills, 86, 105
Bernardsville, 198, 207
Biddle, Nicholas, 45, 47
Big Bend, 11, 135
Bingham, Rudolfus, 69
Binghamton, 51, 53, 61, 62, 96, 97, 136, 140, 142, 164
"Binghamton" (ferryboat), 194, 195
Blair, James, 34, 35, 55
Blair, John Insley, 34, 35, 42, 43, 44, 45, 48, 55, 69, 70, 71, 72, 81, 82, 83, 84, 87, 88, 90, 92, 95, 96, 97, 106, 114, 117, 118, 125
Blair, Marcus, 68
Bliss, George, 87, 90, 97
Bloomfield, 200, 206
Bloomfield, Joseph, 206
Blue Mountains, 80
Boonton, 201, 204
Botany Woolen Mills, 205
Bottled Hill Tavern, 202
Bowman, Rev. Samuel, 22
Boyden, Obadiah, 75, 77
Boyden, Seth, 75, 76
Braddock, General, 10
Brady, Edward L., 193
Brant, David, 202
Brick Church, 78
Bridesville, 82
Brighton Marine Repair Yard, 197
Brisbin, 164
Brisbin, John, 87, 88, 90, 125